Veronica L. Winsel
4 September 1993
Dallas, Texas

VIRGINIA WOOLF

Paper Darts

VIRGINIA WOOLF

Paper Darts

Selected and introduced by Frances Spalding

COLLINS & BROWN

HALF-TITLE: One of a sequence of photographs of Virginia Woolf taken in 1903 by the Edwardian Society photographer, G. C. Beresford.

FRONTISPIECE: *Conversation Piece* by Vanessa Bell, painted in 1911–12 in her Post-Impressionist manner. Conversation was not merely an enjoyable means of communication for the Bloomsbury group but also the means by which its members worked out their philosophy of life.

195 Knightsbridge
London SW7 1RE

A CIP catalogue record for this book is available from the British Library

ISBN 1 85585 046 X

Conceived, edited and designed by Collins & Brown

General Editor : Gabrielle Townsend
Editor : Sarah Hoggett
Picture Research : Philippa Lewis
Art Director : Roger Bristow
Designed by : Ruth Hope

Filmset by Tradespools Ltd, Frome, Somerset
Reproduction by La Cromolito, Milan, Italy
Printed and bound in Great Britain by Clays Ltd, Bungay, Suffolk

CONTENTS

LEFT: *Virginia Woolf by Man Ray, photographer and Surrealist. This photograph was taken in 1935, by which time Virginia was firmly established as a woman of letters.*

INTRODUCTION

FIFTY YEARS AFTER her death Virginia Woolf remains a writer of outstanding rank, one of the most brilliant essayists and novelists of this century. Relatively few essays survive beyond the period for which they were written, but hers continue to hold attention with their mellifluous prose and enlightened, independent point of view. Erudite but never laboured, they are written in a conversational style that is spirited, often humorous and alert to the unexpected. As the author of fiction she is still more acclaimed. Renowned as an innovator, she gradually demolished accepted conceptions of plot and character, promoting in their place a roving, glancing consciousness capable of dealing with the myriad impressions that chase through the mind in any one day. Her desire to pin down the fleeting and evanescent made still more imperative her need to rethink the shape of the novel, to find new structures that would give design and coherence to the narrative and which would replace traditional props. She experimented variously but retained her core ambition to rid the novel of circumstantial clutter and reinstate human nature at its centre.

In her letters we meet this gifted wordsmith off duty, spinning phrases freely and spontaneously for her own pleasure and that of others. Her wide reading had left her aware that letter writing is an art that can be practised, polished and extended. When Clive Bell invited her to comment on his own letters, she advised him to put his style more to the gallop and to try to grasp things that are just out of one's reach. Her own letters reveal a growing increase in confidence, flexibility, subtlety and nuance, as well as a gradual quickening of pace. She wrote at speed, deliberately, while the imprint of the emotion, mood, conversation or event was still fresh in her mind. The impression is gained that nothing must bore or tire.

INTRODUCTION

RIGHT: *An example of Virginia Woolf's distinctive script, for which she always used steel-nibbed pens.*

Virginia's letters shift easily from one topic to the next, touching on things with laughter and affection, but hinting now and then at the tragedy of life and the imperfections of human nature. Immediacy was paramount: 'A true letter', she insisted, 'should be as a film of wax pressed close to the graving in the mind'.

She was familiar with the models provided by past practitioners of this art and admired, in particular, the letters of Jane Welsh Carlyle. Both women wrote animatedly about the idiosyncracies of human character and behaviour discovered, not so much in large acts, but in everyday life and the exacerbation caused by domestic trivia. Mrs Carlyle's delight in diversity led her to remark, 'instead of boiling up individuals into the species, I would draw a chalk circle round every individuality and preach to it to keep within that and cultivate its identity'. Similarly, in Virginia Woolf's correspondence,

FAMILY TREE

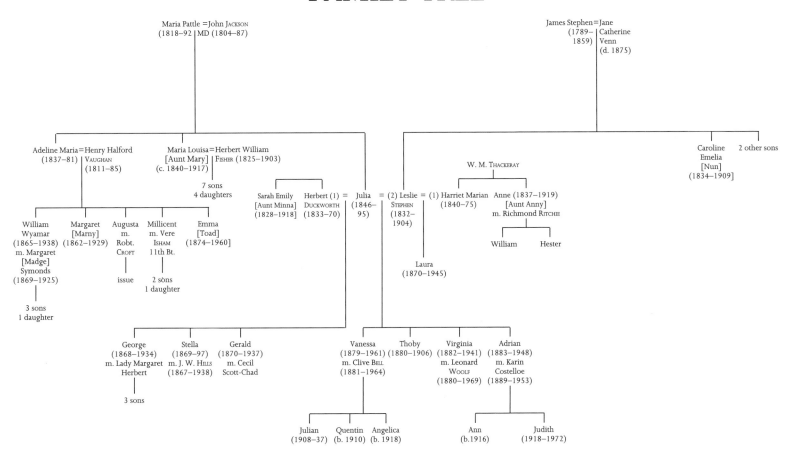

Maria Pattle = John JACKSON
(1818–92 | MD (1804–87)
1859)

James Stephen = Jane
(1789– | Catherine
1859) Venn
(d. 1875)

Adeline Maria = Henry Halford
(1837–81) VAUGHAN
(1811–85)

Maria Louisa = Herbert William
[Aunt Mary] FISHER (1825–1903)
(c. 1840–1917)

Caroline
Emelia
[Nun]
(1834–1909)

2 other sons

7 sons
4 daughters

W. M. THACKERAY

William
Wyamar
(1865–1938)
m. Margaret
[Madge]
Symonds
(1869–1925)

Margaret
[Marny]
(1862–1929)

Augusta
m.
Robt.
CROFT

issue

Millicent
m. Vere
ISHAM
11th Bt.

2 sons
1 daughter

Emma
[Toad]
(1874–1960]

Sarah Emily
[Aunt Minna]
(1828–1918)

Herbert (1) =
DUCKWORTH
(1833–70)

Julia
(1846–
95)

= (2) Leslie = (1) Harriet Marian
STEPHEN   (1840–75)
(1832–
1904)

Anne (1837–1919)
[Aunt Anny]
m. Richmond RITCHIE

William   Hester

Laura
(1870–1945)

3 sons
1 daughter

George
(1868–1934)
m. Lady Margaret
Herbert

Stella
(1869–97)
m. J. W. HILLS
(1867–1938)

Gerald
(1870–1937)
m. Cecil
Scott-Chad

Vanessa
(1879–1961)
m. Clive BELL
(1881–1964)

Thoby
(1880–1906)

Virginia
(1882–1941)
m. Leonard
WOOLF
(1880–1969)

Adrian
(1883–1948)
m. Karin
Costelloe
(1889–1953)

3 sons

Julian
(1908–37)

Quentin
(b. 1910)

Angelica
(b. 1918)

Ann
(b.1916)

Judith
(1918–1972)

huge pleasure is obtained by her from the particularities that characterize the individual to whom she is writing. She pounces on these personal details, at times giving them exaggerated emphasis, and in this way conjures up in the mind of the reader a vivid image of her recipient. This imaginative empathy with others, she believed, is crucial both to the writing and reading of epistolary exchange. 'The way to get into letters', she wrote, 'is to be interested in other people.'

It must have been flattering to her correspondents to find themselves so vividly present in her choice of gossip, teasing or fantasy. Virginia Woolf's ability to adapt her tone of voice suggests that with each of her correspondents she reinvented her character, chameleon-like, in order to be able to communicate better. If this enhanced the sense of intimacy between sender and receiver, its cumulative effect is to suggest that her letters do not speak from the centre as they do in the case of other great imaginative artists, notably Keats. As she herself at one point observes: 'so by creating and being created one swims along never knowing the truth about anything.' But this relativity vanishes the moment she concerns herself with ideas that touch the nub of her being. Her letter to Gerald Brenan, written on Christmas Day 1922, for example, comes direct from the heart.

The sheer quantity of her correspondence – almost four thousand letters have survived loss or destruction – means that this selection can act as no more than a sample to the whole. It will, however, illumine some of the qualities found in greater abundance both in Joanne Trautmann's selection (Congenial Spirits: The Letters of Virginia Woolf) and in the six volumes of collected letters edited by her and Nigel Nicolson. The reader will also be introduced to the handful of recipients who occupy centre stage in Virginia Woolf's correspondence, as well as to others who either remained just off-centre or who form part of the phalanx of individual recipients at which this selection can only hint. One of the fascinations offered by these letters is the entree they provide, not only into the intimate circle of friendships that composed Bloomsbury, but also to a looser circle of acquaintances which includes many names of significance in the variously interlocking arenas created by the arts and society.

Having suffered her first nervous breakdown at the age of thirteen,

ABOVE: Grey Leaves *by Vanessa Bell. After her Post-Impressionist period, Vanessa Bell returned to a more traditional style. She practised her art as a colourist on still lifes and interiors and had a particular love of flowers. The garden at Charleston, her Sussex home, was filled each year with flowers, the result of her avid reading of seed catalogues.*

RIGHT: Still Life with Fruit and Coffee Pot *by Duncan Grant, 1914, an example of his ability to transform mundane objects into a brilliant tapestry of colour.*

INTRODUCTION

LEFT: Study for the Memoir Club by *Vanessa Bell. A preliminary oil sketch for a group portrait celebrating the Memoir Club. Formed in the hope that it would draw from Desmond MacCarthy the novel he never produced, the Club first met to hear a paper read in February 1920. It tapped a rich vein of autobiographical writing and continued to meet irregularly until 1964. At the time that Vanessa Bell began work towards her group portrait, three of the Club's members had died: Roger Fry, Lytton Strachey and Virginia Woolf. Their past role in the Club is acknowledged by the portraits that appear on the wall behind.*

Virginia Woolf lived most of her life under the threat of returning insanity. At various periods she was protected by others from anything that would put a strain on her health. And as her career developed she herself felt an increased need to preserve herself from pressures that would diminish her creative energy. Though she led an animated social life, friends took trouble not to intrude upon her. As a result her relationships with people were often deepened not by conversation but by letter, with the result that she lived more fully in her correspondence than most people.

What is missing in her letters are her more intimate thoughts on the development of her work. These cogitations, together with the doubts, anxieties and recurring depression that she experienced as an artist, she confined to her diaries. But if her letters, for the most part, effervesce with the thoughts and feelings that ran through the surface of her mind, they gain in poignancy and pointedness owing to the fact that they are directed at particular individuals. She must have been aware, given her own achievement and that of many of her friends, that her letters would one day invite publication. But this did not lessen the haste with which she wrote or her method of attack. What happened to her letters posthumously was not her concern. She did not wish any to be published in her lifetime and when Dame Ethel Smyth thought of incorporating examples of their correspondence into one of her books, Virginia protested. 'Let's leave the letters till we're both dead,' she urged. 'That's my plan. I don't keep or destroy but collect miscellaneous bundles of odds and ends, and let posterity, if there is one, burn or not. Lets forget all about death and all about Posterity.'

ABOVE: Dust jacket for A Writer's Diary. *Virginia Woolf began keeping a diary at the age of fourteen. However, not until she was in her thirties did it become a regular habit. After her death Leonard Woolf published selected passages from her diaries under the title A Writer's Diary. Like all her books printed by the Hogarth Press, it bore a dust jacket designed by Vanessa Bell.*

Vanessa Stephen Stella Duckworth Virginia Stephen

HYDE PARK GATE

LEFT: *The Stephen sisters, Vanessa (left) and Virginia (right) with their half-sister, Stella Duckworth, c. 1896. After Stella's tragically early death her widower, Jack Hills, drew close to Vanessa, who seemed to return his affection. Their burgeoning relationship was opposed by Stella's socially ambitious half-brother, George Duckworth, for not only would such a liaison provoke gossip in Society, but marriage to one's dead wife's sister was illegal at that time.*

RIGHT: *Julia Stephen was the second wife of Leslie Stephen and was herself a widow when she married him. Her concern for others extended beyond her immediate family to such an extent that Virginia Woolf once reflected: 'Can I remember ever being alone with her for more than a few minutes? Someone was always interrupting'.*

WHEN THESE LETTERS begin Virginia Woolf is still Virginia Stephen, aged nineteen, and living with her family at 22 Hyde Park Gate in Kensington. She has two elder siblings, Vanessa and Thoby, and one younger brother, Adrian. There are also two elder half-brothers living at home, George and Gerald, the children of her mother Julia Stephen's first marriage to Herbert Duckworth. A third child of this union, Stella, had died young, in 1897, a few months after her marriage to Jack Hills. This tragedy had followed hard upon another, for in 1895 Julia Stephen had died, aged forty-nine.

Virginia was thirteen at the time of her mother's death and soon afterwards underwent what appears to have been a nervous breakdown, the first evidence of her mental instability. She recovered only to suffer a relapse after Stella died. Towards the end of her life she referred to the years 1897 to 1904 as the time when 'the lash of a random unheeding flail ... pointlessly and brutally killed the two people who should, normally and naturally, have made those years, not perhaps happy but normal and natural'. Denied maternal love, she was left with an idealized memory of her mother which remained for many years an overshadowing presence in her life. She eventually obtained release from it by analyzing and celebrating her mother in prose, as Mrs Ramsay in *To the Lighthouse*.

The deaths of her mother and Stella deepened further her dependence on Vanessa, the two sisters having formed an alliance in childhood. Rivalry was diminished by the tacit agreement that one sister was to become a painter, the other a writer. It was a demarcation that helped foster their solidarity. Their mutual dependence was initially protective. It helped both cope with the uneasy circumstances that prevailed after their mother's death. They were

ABOVE: Thoby Stephen photographed by G.C. Beresford, from a sequence of four found in *Vanessa Bell's photograph album.*

also united in their desire to resist the demands of Edwardian society, for whilst Leslie Stephen mourned the loss of his wife, George Duckworth assumed a paternal role and insisted that both sisters should enter the social round. Both George and his brother Gerald were essentially well-meaning, but their confused feelings towards their half-sisters led to fondlings and fumblings that on at least one occasion became sexual in intent. In this instance it was Gerald who erred, though it was George whose embraces were the most persistent.

The Stephen sisters were educated at home, unlike their brothers who were sent away to school and afterwards went up to Cambridge. Virginia envied them both, but especially Thoby whom she describes at one point as 'a Greek God . . . rather too massive for the drawing room'. Adrian, on the other hand, she tended to disparage. 'Adrian babbles away,' she wrote in 1903, '15 years younger than all the rest of us. He grows too fast to think or feel, or do anything but eat.' Not surprisingly it was Thoby on whom she chose to test out her ideas on literature.

More remote, though equally important to her, was her father, Leslie Stephen, the eminent journalist, philosopher, author and editor of the *Dictionary of National Biography*. One of his gifts to his daughter was the free run of his library. 'Gracious child, how you gobble!', Leslie Stephen remarked, for even he was surprised at the amount she read. Virginia recognized as a child that she had greater affinity with her father than with her mother, but as an old man he was not always easy to love. He could become unreasonably irascible, self-pitying, tyrannical and demanding. To a large extent the routine of the house revolved around him, and after Julia Stephen's and Stella's deaths it fell to Vanessa and Virginia to attend to his tea-time visitors. This daily custom obliged them to develop a certain manner, for conversation had to be intelligent but light. At the tea table Virginia developed a tone of voice which she later recognized, and to an extent resented, in her essays.

In the spring of 1902, the same year that he received a knighthood, Leslie Stephen was discovered to have abdominal cancer. He was operated on in December, but his strength gradually diminished, and in April 1903 it became clear that the disease was spreading. Vanessa was told that Sir Leslie had not long to live; she thought it best that he should – if possible – be kept in ignorance of the seriousness of his condition. As the following letters reveal, his dying drew to the fore Virginia's love and respect for him. During this melancholy time of delayed crisis, her letters also give voice to unexpectedly jubilant remarks. Even before Leslie Stephen died in February 1904, his children had begun looking for a house in Bloomsbury, aware that as one chapter of their family life ended another was about to begin.

TO THOBY STEPHEN

[October? 1901]   22 Hyde Park Gate, S.W.

My dear Thoby,

I dont know whether I imagined it, or whether you once did say really that you wanted a kitten for your rooms. Anyhow, if you do I could send you in a hamper a very nice black kitten with signs of distinguished birth about it—and a charming and lovable disposition (like mine!) I have been offered it by Miss Power, but my room apparently would not suit it, as it ought to be able to get out of doors—which it could do in your rooms.

However, I am afraid you will be able to get a Cambridge kitten (if you want one) without this bother of sending it. Only could you let me know as soon as you get this?

[38]   Yr. Goat

Miss Power was teaching Virginia bookbinding. 'Goat' was Virginia's nickname.

ABOVE: *Sir Leslie Stephen, father of Virginia. Leslie was descended from a line of upper-middle-class liberals, the legacy of whose intellectual and social concerns no doubt helped shape the radical opinions of Bloomsbury.*

HYDE PARK GATE

LEFT: Old Silver Street Bridge, Cambridge, a woodcut by Gwen Raverat. Several members of Bloomsbury originally met as undergraduates at Cambridge. Various qualities often associated with this university town were also characteristic of Bloomsbury, notably intellectual honesty, austerity and a certain unworldliness of outlook.

HYDE PARK GATE

TO VIOLET DICKINSON

[4 May? 1903]   [22 Hyde Park Gate, S.W.]

My Beloved Woman,

Your letters come like balm on the heart. I really think I must do what I never have done—try to keep them. I've never kept a single letter all my life—but this romantic friendship ought to be preserved. Very few people have any feelings to express—at least of affection or sympathy—and if those that do feel dont express—the worlds so much more like a burnt out moon—cold living for the Sparroys and Violets. This is because you think, or say, you oughtn't to write nice hot letters. Kitty never pierces my tough hide, or tries to. She came to see father the other day, the first time since his illness, and asked him why he hadn't been to call on her, all this time, which was rather *too* fashionable, I thought. And didnt volunteer more than a fishy white glove to *me*—perhaps naturally—only this explains why in crises of emotion, Violet is the Sympathetic Sink, not Kitty.

All Stephen's are self centred by nature; taking more than giving—but if you once understand that, and it cant be helped you can get on all right with them. Indeed some of them are really rather loveable people. . . .

Nothing has happened here. Nurse says father oughtn't even now, to go to the study, but he had better try, if he wants to. As yet he has stayed downstairs. Georgie is writing to Seton to say *we* are anxious for Treves, if it can be managed without worrying father. Seton apparently is really anxious for a thorough examination—and father refuses to let Seton touch him.

Come on Wed: 5.

[80]   Sparroy

ABOVE: *Violet Dickinson with Clive Bell and his two sons, Julian and Quentin, at Asheham in 1912. These and other photographs in this book have been taken from Vanessa Bell's photograph album.*

Kitty (Maxse, née Lushington) was a family friend greatly admired by Virginia who gradually, however, perceived a coldness behind her fashionable beauty. She became the original for Virginia Woolf's eponymous character, Mrs Dalloway. Dr Seton was the family physician. Sir Frederick Treves was Surgeon Extraordinary to Queen Victoria, 1900-1901. Sparroy was a nickname used of herself by Virginia only in her letters to Violet. Its origin is unknown but it is suggestive of some bird or animal, bedraggled and in need of care.

TO THOBY STEPHEN

[May 1903]   [22 Hyde Park Gate, S.W.]

My dear Cresty,

It seems about time that I should write to you, and that you should write to me—But there aint much news to tell you—We have just had Nun's visit—which, as you can imagine, was not cheerful. After half an hours talk one begins to wish that there were a way invented of stopping her. She seems to work round in a circle—But she is pathetic! Are you to write for Trevelyan? Jack has a very strong opinion that you ought to go to the Bar—He says it wouldn't be so very expensive—and youre made for a Judge—I wish you would—You would give judgments uninfluenced by emotion I know—and if I had reason on my side, you should be my lawyer. Should you like it better than Treasury or Colonial Office? I dont get anybody to argue with me now, and feel the want. I have to delve from books, painfully and all alone, what you get every evening sitting over your fire and smoking your pipe with Strachey etc. No wonder my knowledge is but scant. Theres nothing like talk as an educator I'm sure. Still I try my best with Shakespeare—I read Sidney Lees Life—What do you think of his sonnet theory? It seems to me a little too like Sidney Lee—all that about Shakespeare's eye to the main chance—his flattery of Southampton etc.—But the Mr W. H. is sensible—I must read the sonnets and find my own opinion. Sidney says that Shakespeare *felt* none of it—I mean that not a word applies to him personally—But it is a satisfactory book—doesn't pretend to make theories—and only gives the most authentic facts.

The Season is beginning—not that that affects *me* much—but George and Gerald are out every night—balls and operas. Nessa and I grub along in our own ways. She has nude models here 3 days a week—and the vigorous [Janet] Case has swept down from Hampstead. Seton was here the other day—He thought father a little weaker than when we went away—but says theres no use in having Treves. It might bother father, and nothing more can be done. Father is very cheerful, and talks away, but he doesn't get up to the study—and cant do much work. He was very much pleased with your letter—and handwriting! I think one of us might see Treves—without telling father—even tho' he cant do anything, he might tell us more.

Dont work too hard—or do anything foolish—and take care of your lovely crest—which must be sadly out of order now—

[81]   Yr. loving, Goat

Nun was a family nickname for Caroline Emelia Stephen, Virginia's Quaker aunt. George Macaulay Trevelyan was a Fellow of Trinity College, Cambridge. Jack (Hills) was the widower of Virginia's half-sister, Stella Duckworth. Janet Case was Virginia's tutor in Greek and a gifted—though strict—teacher. Virginia learnt a great deal from her, and these lessons marked the start of a lifelong friendship. Virginia kept in touch with her and occasionally visited Janet and her sister in Hampstead. Leslie Stephen was now so ill that Vanessa Stephen gave up art school and employed models to pose for her at home.

To Violet Dickinson

Thursday night [31 December 1903]   22 Hyde Park Gate, S.W.

My Violet,

Wilson thought Father weaker this morning—his pulse not so good. His temp. has been 100 all day; at 2 AM. it goes up to 102. Wilson thinks the temp. may go down as it did before—but I dont know whether father will be able to live through the weakness which must come afterwards. He has been asleep most of today, very quietly. He sleeps more and more, but is perfectly conscious when he wakes, I think he gets weaker every day—and he takes nothing but a little milk and meatjuice, and that with difficulty. But in a way I feel happier about him—he is less able to think and to worry—and that is the worst thing. But however you look at it, it is a miserable time. If he had died at first it would have been easier, but now one has to give up more—I mean all these days he has been there, and able to talk a little, and one has had time to think—however, I know I shall be glad for him.

We have been tramping Bloomsbury this afternoon with Beatrice, and staring up at dingy houses. There are lots to be had—but Lord how dreary! It seems so far away, and so cold and gloomy—but that was due to the dark and the cold I expect. Really we shall never get a house we like so well as this, but it is better to go.

We are the sanest family in London and talk and laugh as though nothing were happening; Adrian and Thoby are going to sing the new year in! We should never get on without this kind of thing.

I write letters all about ourselves. Dont really hurry back because of us. It will make your husband angry, and there's no real reason except that we want you, which isnt sufficient.

The nurses are rather bothersome, but have now settled to dignity and silence, which is peaceful at anyrate. Traill is depressed, I think a little tired of it all.

[145]   Yr. AVS

As Leslie Stephen grew steadily weaker, doctors and nurses became daily visitors to the house. Wilson was the doctor sent by Leslie Stephen's surgeon, Hugh Rigby. Traill was a nurse. Lady Beatrice Thynne was a family friend and the daughter of Lady Bath. The allusion to Violet's husband is an often-made joke on Virginia's part, for Violet never married.

ABOVE: Nurse Traill, Thoby Stephen, Susan Lushington, George Duckworth, Virginia and Vanessa Stephen in 1903.

RIGHT: Sir Leslie Stephen and his daughter Virginia. This photograph was taken by G.C. Beresford shortly before Sir Leslie's death. Virginia's intense grief at his death, mingled with guilt at her impatience with his irascibility in old age, contributed to the serious mental breakdown she suffered in May 1904.

TO JANET CASE

[February 1904]   22 Hyde Park Gate, S.W.

Dear Miss Case,

Father is very weak, and has a great deal of fever, but he is without actual pain. He has so much vitality—but they can do nothing. He is quite conscious when you speak to him, and talks as he always did. He asked me today when you were coming, and what I was reading. But he is fearfully tired. Thank you for your letter. I dont think there is any good in going through these things—and it is all pure loss. But that one realises afterwards. You see I'm not in a pious frame of mind!

But we have all been so happy together and there never was anybody so loveable.

[155]   Yr. aff. AVS

TO JANET CASE

Tuesday night [23 February 1904]   22 Hyde Park Gate, S.W.

Dear Miss Case,

It [the funeral] is to be tomorrow at 3 at Golders Green. We shall go.

Father died very peacefully, as we sat by him. I know it was what he wanted most. Nothing now can hurt him, and that is what one has dreaded.

But how to go on without him, I dont know. All these years we have hardly been apart, and I want him every moment of the day. But we still have each other—Nessa and Thoby and Adrian and I, and when we are together he and Mother do not seem far off.

[165]   Yr. aff. AVS

TO CHARLES ELIOT NORTON

13th March 1904   [Manorbier, Pembrokeshire]

My dear Mr Norton,

You will of course have heard long ago of Father's death, but I should like to tell you that it was in every way the end that we wished for him. He was talking to us all on Sunday morning in his most vigorous and cheerful way—about books and people—and saying that he felt less tired than usual. He also saw a friend and she was amazed at his strength and interest in everything. Half an hour afterwards he became unconscious, at least he did not know us though he talked to himself constantly. This was on Sunday afternoon—All that evening he grew weaker, apparently without any pain—and he died at 7 on Monday morning so peacefully that one could only feel happy for him.

His dread always was lest he should lose his power of thinking, or should have to suffer pain. Of course all through this long illness he was often very tired and weak, but he had no actual pain, and his mind never seemed clearer or more brilliant. He was able to read on the last morning of his life, asking me to bring him an article on Shakespeare and a new poem by Thomas Hardy—and almost every day he saw two or three friends. Even though he was so ill I think this last year of his life was a happy one; he seemed so peaceful and glad—almost surprised—at the love of all his friends and the admiration which people have shown him more than ever before. I think there was no one so loveable. He often talked of you, and enjoyed every letter you sent him. Your letters, he told me, were some of the very few he cared to keep, and he gave me each as it came to add to the others. The last you wrote reached us after his death, and I have put it with the rest. I do not know if you have any photograph of him or would like to have one. We had several taken just before his operation in December 1902. They are, I think, as good as photographs can be, though he looks more ill than he did afterwards. I will send you one, in case you may like it.

[172]   Your affectionate, Virginia Stephen

Charles Eliot Norton was Professor of History of Art at Harvard University. His friendship with Leslie Stephen began during a visit Stephen made to America whilst writing journalism on the Federal Cause in America.

BLOOMSBURY

LEFT: *Saxon Sydney-Turner by Vanessa Bell, c. 1908. Sydney-Turner was the most silent member of Bloomsbury yet his comments, when made, were acute and often slightly acid. In 1909, Virginia accompanied him and her brother Adrian to Bayreuth, where she observed: 'Saxon is dormant all day, and rather peevish if you interrupt him. He hops along, before or behind, swinging his ugly stick, and humming, like a stridulous grasshopper'.*

SIR LESLIE STEPHEN died on 22 February 1904 and his funeral was held two days later. Released from the gloom that had been cast over their home by his failing health, the Stephen children went on holiday, first to Manorbier in Pembrokeshire and then to Venice and Florence. On their return they stopped at Paris and there Virginia experienced, in the company they kept and the conversations they pursued, a freedom that exhilarated her.

Immediately on her return to London, however, Virginia suffered another serious breakdown. She was kept away from London for some months, whilst her sister, Vanessa, moved the Stephen family into their new home, 46 Gordon Square, in Bloomsbury. Virginia, lodged with Violet Dickinson at Welwyn, then with her Quaker aunt, Caroline Emelia Stephen, at Cambridge, and elsewhere, was eager to return to her life in London. Once back she began teaching adult-education classes in English literature and history at Morley College. With encouragement from Violet Dickinson, she tried her hand at journalism, writing articles and reviews. She also began to experiment with descriptive essays and had since 1897 been intermittently keeping a journal. As a writer, she quickly began to enjoy success and by 1905 was reviewing regularly for The Times Literary Supplement.

Once settled in Gordon Square, the Stephens began holding 'at homes' on Thursday evenings. These played a crucial role in the formation of Bloomsbury, a term that came to be used not only of an area, but also of this group of individuals united by a common attitude to life and by friendship. At first these 'at homes' attracted an uncomfortable mix of old and new acquaintances, but gradually the former fell away, leaving a nucleus of Thoby's Cambridge friends, including Clive Bell, Maynard Keynes, the critic Desmond MacCarthy, E. M. Forster, Saxon Sydney-Turner, Lytton Strachey

ABOVE: Hotel Garden in Florence *by Vanessa Bell, 1909. Virginia and Vanessa first visited Florence in 1904, shortly after Sir Leslie Stephen's death, and returned there in 1909 with Vanessa's husband, Clive.*

and his cousin, the painter Duncan Grant. Owing to his friendship with Thoby Stephen and others at Cambridge, Leonard Woolf, who left England to undertake colonial service in 1904, automatically assumed a role within Bloomsbury on his return from Ceylon in 1911. Likewise the painter and critic, Roger Fry, though he did not enter Bloomsbury until 1910, was swiftly absorbed into its innermost core. The chief philosophical influence on their thought was G. E. Moore's *Principia Ethica*, which promoted the belief that 'personal affections and aesthetic enjoyments include all the greatest, and by far the greatest, goods we can imagine'.

Bloomsbury made a significant contribution to the development of liberal thought. In their desire to replace hypocrisy and cant with an attitude to life that was free, rational and civilized, they focused attention on the near at hand. They began by overturning the Victorian emphasis on public duty in favour of persistent analysis and evaluation of personal relationships. This encouraged a self-consciousness and attentiveness which enabled them to gain great pleasure and strength from the intimate circle that Bloomsbury represented. 'Where they seem to me to triumph,' Virginia explained in a letter to a friend in 1925, 'is in having worked out a view of life which was not by any means corrupt or sinister or merely intellectual; rather ascetic and austere indeed; which still holds, and keeps them dining together, and staying together, after 20 years; and no amount of quarrelling or success, or failure has altered this. Now I do think this rather creditable.'

TO VIOLET DICKINSON

[6? May 1904]   [Paris]

My Violet,

I discovered a letter written to you, but not sent. It was in my pocket all the time, when it should have been sending shocks and thrills through a maiden bosom in [Welwyn] Hertfordshire. We have had our Beatrice [Thynne] and she has flashed across us, and disappeared, leaving us rather gaping. She stayed exactly two days, in which she managed many more sights than you ever did, and preached like the valiant old Heathen she is.

ABOVE: Lytton Strachey, by Dora Carrington. Strachey had been one of Thoby Stephen's circle at Cambridge, and later became one of Virginia's closest friends. She greatly valued his 'wit and infinite intelligence'.

ABOVE: Duncan Grant, 1913. Duncan was largely brought up in London by the Strachey family. His many affairs were mostly with his own sex, but just before the First World War he entered into a relationship with Vanessa Bell that lasted until her death.

She is red and tough as a very fine apple; her face is positively muscular, with character which seems to have stiffened there. We took her to dine with [Clive] Bell last night, a real Bohemian party, after her heart. Kelly the painter was there, and we stayed talking of Art, Sculpture and Music till 11.30. This was all in the common cafe, while we smoked half a dozen cigarettes a piece. Kelly is an enthusiast, and Beatrice seeing this contradicted him. She expounded theories on Wagner which were, I know, made that moment. He actually shook his fist at her across the table, and at one moment I held her down—a stormy scene.

She left early this morning . . . . Now we go and see Rodins studio tomorrow morning, with Bell and Kelly—and that is our last expedition! Oh Lord, how cross I have been, how dull, how tempersome,—and am still. You had much to stand: I wish I could repay all the bad times with good times. There should be some system of repayment in this world—you believe in a next, I know, for that purpose. Oh my Violet if you could only find me a great solid bit of work to do when I get back that will make me forget my own stupidity I should be so grateful. I must work. We leave early on Monday. . . .

Keep well. Both nieces will never forget all you did for them.

[178]   Yr AVS

Gerald Kelly, a follower of Whistler, later became a polished society portraitist, his paintings growing duller as he became more eminent. He earned himself a knighthood and the Presidency of the Royal Academy.

TO VIOLET DICKINSON

30 Sept. [1904]   Manor House, Teversal [Nottinghamshire]

My Violet,

. . . I am longing to begin work. I know I can write, and one of these days I mean to produce a good book. What do you think? Life interests me intensely, and writing is I know my natural means of expression. I dont feel up to much, as far as my brain goes. At least I soon get tired of reading, and

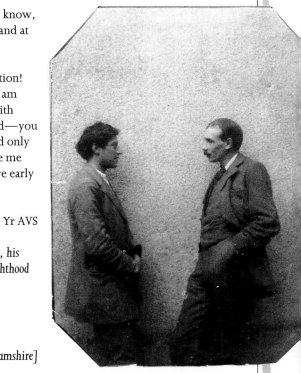

ABOVE: *Duncan Grant and Maynard Keynes, 1912. Keynes, who became one of the most influential economists of this century, succeeded Strachey as one of Duncan Grant's lovers.*

I haven't tried to write, more than letters. I have a headache at this moment, so I wont go on.

I have taken to smoking a pipe, which the doctor thinks an excellent thing, and I find it very soothing.

Oh my Violet, I do want Father so—and yet I am very happy in a way.
[183]   Your loving AVS

TO VIOLET DICKINSON

30th Oct: [1904]   *The Porch, Cambridge*

My Violet,

I was very glad of your letter. Nessa's visit was delightful, and we talked the whole time, not on altogether soothing subjects though. I cant make her, or you, or anybody, see that it is a great hardship to me to have to spend two more long months wandering about in other peoples comfortless houses, when I have my own house [Gordon Square] waiting for me and rent paid regular on Quarter day. It is such a natural thing from an outsiders point of view, that I get only congratulations, and people say how lucky I am, and how glad I ought to be to be out of London. They dont realise that London means my own home, and books, and pictures, and music, from all of which I have been parted since February now,—and I have never spent such a wretched 8 months in my life. And yet that tyrannical, and as I think, shortsighted Savage insists upon another two. I told him when I saw him that the only place I can be quiet and free is in my home, with Nessa: she understands my moods, and lets me alone in them, whereas with strangers like Nun I have to explain every random word—and it is so exhausting. I long for a large room to myself, with books and nothing else, where I can shut myself up, and see no one, and read myself into peace. This would be possible at Gordon Sq: and nowhere else. I wonder why Savage doesn't see this. As a matter of fact my sleep hasn't improved a scrap since I have been here, and his sleeping draught gives me a headache, and nothing else. However I shall have a few days in London next week, which will be some relief, and meanwhile I can let off

ABOVE: The Bedroom, Gordon Square, *by Vanessa Bell, 1912.*

BLOOMSBURY

LEFT: 46 Gordon Square, by
Vanessa Bell, probably painted in
1909–10. Bloomsbury was a less
fashionable area than Kensington where
the Stephen family grew up. The move to
this area had caused protest among some
friends of the family.

my irritation upon you! Nessa contrived to say that it didn't much matter to anyone, her included, I suppose, whether I was here or in London, which made me angry, but then she has a genius for stating unpleasant truths in her matter of fact voice! . . .

[186]   Yr. AVS

Dr Savage was the family doctor. Nun was Virginia's nickname for her aunt, the Quaker Caroline Emelia Stephen, in whose home she was convalescing.

TO VIOLET DICKINSON

Nov. 9th [1905]   *46 Gordon Square*

My Violet,

. . . I have had such a run of work as is not remembered for I cant say how many years; books from the Times, the Academy, the Guardian—it must be confessed that I write great nonsense, but you will understand that I have to make money to pay my bills. The Quaker wont see it; and talks with deep significance of *serious* work not *pot boilers*. Really I have almost more reviewing than I feel to be quite moral; but I manage some Greek and good English in between.

Then Nessa has fairly got her [Friday] Club started; and they are to have an Exhibition at once, and you will just be in time to go with me to see it. Really that gives me quite a thrill. I have been friendless so long that I shall suddenly feel respectable. Shall I buy a new hat to celebrate your return? I tell you an emphatic red line is drawn under Dec: 3rd in my calendar.

Nessa has written you so many sheets that I suppose I may be as foolish as I like here. Then we have our Thursdays; your husband came to one, in the midst of discussion upon the birth place of Jesus Christ; the little poets were rather afraid of his evening dress, and huddled together in corners like moping owls. But he was very good for them.

Then on Wednesdays I have my English Composition; 10 people: 4 men 6 women. It is I suppose the most useless class in the College; and so Sheepshanks thinks. She sat through the whole lesson last night; and almost stamped with impatience. But what can I do? I have an old Socialist of 50, who thinks he must bring the Parasite (the Aristocrat, that is you and Nelly) into an essay upon Autumn; and a Dutchman who thinks—at the end of the class too—that I have been teaching him Arithmetic; and anaemic shop girls who say they would write more but they only get an hour for their dinner, and there doesn't seem much time for writing. Adrian started a Greek class; which lived for two lessons, and came to an end last night. Oh Morley College is a fine place and—can you end the quotation? . . .

What fragment of your body will be thrown to me among the howling crowd of your friends? The widening of your mind has been a painful discipline. Dont buy me things: come back well and affectionate.

[251]   Yr. AVS

The Friday Club, founded by Vanessa who was inspired by the conviviality among artists she had experienced in Paris, met to hear papers read and eventually began mounting regular exhibitions. Virginia observed it with amusement ('one half of the committee shriek Whistler and French impressionists, and the other are stalwart British'). The habitués of the Thursday 'at homes' had, in the summer of 1905, produced a privately printed collection of poems entitled Euphrosyne; hence Virginia's reference to 'the little poets'. Nelly (Lady Robert Cecil) was a friend of the Stephen family. Mary Sheepshanks, Principal of Morley College, had invited Virginia to give classes in literature and history. The courses were for working people wanting to improve their education.

TO MADGE VAUGHAN

[June? 1906]   46 Gordon Square, Bloomsbury

My dearest Madge,

I feel rather guilty to have made you write so much and read so much in the midst of everything else. But I am most grateful, and that I hope you will believe.

I do agree with every word you say, and I think I understand your meaning. My only defence is that I write of things as I see them; and I am quite conscious all the time that it is a very narrow, and rather bloodless point of view. I think . . . I could explain a little why this is so from external reasons; such as education, way of life etc. And so perhaps I may get something better as I grow older. George Eliot was near 40 I think, when she wrote her first novel . . . the Scenes [of *Clerical Life*].

But my present feeling is that this vague and dream like world, without love, or heart, or passion, or sex, is the world I really care about, and find interesting. For, though they are dreams to you, and I cant express them at all adequately, these things are perfectly real to me.

But please dont think for a moment that I am satisfied, or think that my view takes in any whole. Only it seems to me better to write of the things I do feel, than to dabble in things I frankly dont understand in the least. That is the kind of blunder—in literature—which seems to me ghastly and unpardonable: people, I mean, who wallow in emotions without understanding them. Then they are merely animal and hideous. But, of course, any great writer treats them so that they are beautiful, and turns statues into men and women. I wonder if you understand my priggish and immature mind at all? The things I sent you were mere experiments; and I shall never try to put them forward as my finished work. They shall sit in a desk till they are burnt! But I am very glad that you were so frank; because I have had so very little criticism upon my work that I really dont know what kind of impression I make. But do please remember, that if I am heartless when I write, I am very sentimental really, only I dont know how to express it, and devoted to you and the babies; and I only want to be treated like a nice child. I do hope you are better.

Shall I send some vegetables? or what do you like out of this vast and wicked town? Please say,

[272]   Yr. loving AVS

I N SEPTEMBER 1906, Virginia travelled to Greece with Vanessa and Violet Dickinson. Thoby and Adrian Stephen had gone on ahead in order to travel the Dalmatian coast on horseback. They all met in Olympia and began touring, moving from one site to the next, until

BLOOMSBURY

LEFT: Adrian Stephen, painted by Duncan Grant at the time of his affair with the sitter. Grant was also to form a lasting relationship with Adrian's sister, Vanessa, after her marital relations with Clive Bell had ended, and was the father of Angelica.

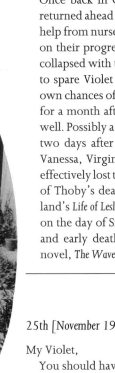

Vanessa fell ill with what appears to have been a physical breakdown. After a fortnight's rest she was well enough to make the journey home. Once back in Gordon Square they discovered that Thoby, who had returned ahead of the rest, was seriously ill with typhoid. Virginia, with help from nurses, took responsibility for both invalids, and sent reports on their progress to Violet Dickinson who, on reaching London, also collapsed with typhoid. Vanessa recovered but Thoby did not. In order to spare Violet Dickinson further anguish, and thereby endanger her own chances of recovery, Virginia did not tell her of Thoby's death and for a month afterwards continued to pretend that he was progressing well. Possibly a part of her could not admit Thoby's death to herself, for two days after he died Clive Bell proposed to and was accepted by Vanessa, Virginia having to come to terms with the fact that she had effectively lost two siblings almost at once. Violet happened on the news of Thoby's death by accident, whilst reading a review of F. W. Maitland's *Life of Leslie Stephen* which commented that the book had appeared on the day of Sir Leslie's elder son's death. Thoby, his character, looks and early death, later inspired the creation of Percival in Virginia's novel, *The Waves*.

LEFT: *Vanessa Bell at Asheham, the small Regency house situated some six miles outside Lewes in Sussex and rented jointly by Virginia and Vanessa, in 1911. In 1912 Virginia wrote from Asheham to Violet Dickinson: '. . . we are very happy here . . . I think it would be nice to leave all ones clothes in a great box in London, and turn into a kind of muddy turnip root.'*

TO VIOLET DICKINSON

25th [November 1906]   46 Gordon Square, Bloomsbury

My Violet,
   You should have had a letter from Nessa before this. She wrote, and I suppose I put it down somewhere, as my habit still is.
   . . . Thoby is going on splendidly. He is very cross with his nurses, because they wont give him mutton chops and beer; and he asks why he cant go for a ride with Bell, and look for wild geese. Then nurse says "wont tame ones do" at which we laugh.
   Nessa also increases steadily. Really I think we are through our troubles—but it has been the devil of a time. I have tried to write—but perpetual sense has consolidated my brains. Thoby has been reading

reviews of the Life [of Leslie Stephen], and wants to know if you are up to that? The dr. says his brain is the strongest he knows; and his heart is fit to do the work of two men. Still, it is a long job, as you have to be so careful with food—and then as his lungs were bad there is the danger of cold—and he is like a child. We hope he will get away in 3 weeks, with Bell; and Nessa will be more than ready to go before that. She is to get up and come down if she likes this week—but I have made her promise to stay more or less in her room till she goes away—at least to make that her headquarters. She really is a wonderful woman. She sat down solidly to get well, confronted all the doctors, and has proved that she was right all the time. She saw Kitty one day, but as a rule she only sees us. They let her do as she thinks fit now; I feel happier about her than I have done for months. She does seem to me rested all through—brain and body—and ready to begin again as fresh as paint.

And now that Thoby is out of danger things will go swimmingly: only my dear old furry one must heal up—and come to a festal dinner . . . [306]   Yr. AVS

Thoby had died five days before this letter was written.

TO VIOLET DICKINSON

[18 December 1906]   46 Gordon Square, Bloomsbury

Beloved Violet,

Do you hate me for telling so many lies? You know we had to do it. You must think that Nessa is *radiantly happy* and Thoby was splendid to the end.

These great things are not terrible, and I know we can still make a good job of it—and we want you more and more. I never knew till this happened how I should turn to you and want you with me when no one else could help.

This is quite true, my beloved Violet, and I must write it down for once. I think of you as one of the people—Adrian is the other—who make it worth while to live and be happy. You are part of all that is best, and

ABOVE: *Clive Bell at Studland Bay, Dorset, where the Bells holidayed in 1910 and 1911.*

happiest in our lives. Thoby was always asking me about you. I know you loved him, and he loved you.

The only thing I feel I could not bear would be to think that this news should make you worse. It would not be right. I can feel happy about him: he was so brave and strong, and his life was perfect.

Now we must be more to each other than ever; and there will be all Nessa's life to look forward to. She is wonderfully well.

"I think on the whole I get happier every day—though it's difficult to think that I can ever be much happier than I have often been at moments during the last few weeks." That is what she writes today.

Beloved, get well and come back to your Wall [Wallaby] who loves you.

[326]   Yr. AVS

ABOVE: *Clive Bell, drawn by Henry Lamb in 1908.*

NOW AGED TWENTY-FIVE, Virginia Stephen was becoming uncomfortably aware that others expected her to marry. She had had a mild flirtation with the poet and classics scholar, Walter Headlam, in 1906, but it had come to nothing. Meanwhile she adjusted herself to the reality of her sister's forthcoming marriage and prepared to move herself and Adrian into a house in Fitzroy Square in order to leave 46 Gordon Square for Vanessa and Clive. She was intrigued and sometimes irritated by her new brother-in-law who shared her literary interests. His critical abilities made her more self-conscious, as some of her early letters to him reveal. She also shared with him her ideas for a novel, initially called *Melymbrosia* but eventually published as *The Voyage Out*.

TO VIOLET DICKINSON

[28? December 1906]   [Lane End, Bank, Lyndhurst, Hampshire]

My Violet,

I am glad you have been up. It is freezing cold here so that Adrian couldn't hunt and we went for a walk instead. Yesterday I lost myself, and got home so sleepy that I couldn't write—but, my word, trees are better than people. I have a long letter from Clive, pompous and polished as usual, but not amusing. He is a careful youth, and realises his own luck which is something. He says his family is ''tiresome''—to which I always feel inclined to say a family is always as good as you deserve. Nobody is ever too good for their own flesh and blood. But he takes pains to show that he sees their limitations.

Why on earth does Nelly say I have a 'steady head'!? and what do you know about the way I have come through these months? I wonder. I am amused by the indiscriminate praise I get; however Walter Headlam will tell me the truth.

I think housekeeping is what I do best, and I mean to run our house on very remarkable lines. Does housekeeping interest you at all? I think it really ought to be just as good as writing, and I never see—as I argued the other day with Nessa—where the separation between the two comes in. At least if you put books on one side and life on t' other, each is a poor and bloodless thing. But my theory is that they mix indistinguishably. . . .
[332]   Yr. AVS

TO VIOLET DICKINSON

[31 December 1906]   Lane End [Bank, Lyndhurst, Hampshire]

My Violet,

This is only a line as I have to write various dull letters before going.

Nessa sounds happier and happier but wants to see us. I have long letters fr. Kitty [Maxse] and George [Duckworth].

The world is full of kindness and stupidity, I wish everyone didn't tell me

ABOVE: *Clive Bell and Virginia Woolf at Studland Bay in 1910. The previous year, at a time when Vanessa was deeply absorbed with her first-born son, Julian, Clive and Virginia had engaged in a brief flirtation whilst all were on holiday at St Ives. It says much for Vanessa's ability to manage human relationships that she did not allow this development to damage the bond between her and her sister.*

to marry. Is it crude human nature breaking out? I call it disgusting. It is thawing now, and the snow is all dirty. I shall be glad to go, and I only wish I was coming back to London and cd. sit with you in the fire light.

I wish I knew how you are. Sleep is the very devil, and drugs are worst of all. I read your Keats all day. O divine!

I will write again.

[334]   Yr. AVS

TO VIOLET DICKINSON

Thursday [3 January 1907]   46 Gordon Square, Bloomsbury

My Violet,

Here we are for the night, passing through. We spent the day at Bath—a Meredithian expedition—so far as Nessa and Clive were concerned. They swung along the streets arm in arm; she had a gauze streamer, red as blood flying over her shoulder, a purple scarf, a shooting cap, tweed skirt and great brown boots. Then her hair swept across her forehead, and she was tawny and jubilant and lusty as a young God. I never saw her look better. Indeed our two days were more of a treat than I expected; I am not unselfish, as you know; but selfishly I do enjoy life and beauty and audacity, and all that freedom and generosity which seem to bathe her like her own proper atmosphere. And Clive as I think I said, is perfectly fit to receive all this; I think he has a very sweet and sincere nature, and capable brains and great artistic sensibility of every kind. What you miss is inspiration of any kind, but then old Nessa is no genius, though she has all the human gifts; and genius is an accident. They are the most honest couple I ever saw; a little more imagination and they would be less scrupulous—but on the whole, I doubt that man and woman are made much better in the world. I did not see Nessa alone, but I realise that that is all over, and I shall never see her alone any more; and Clive is a new part of her, which I must learn to accept.

Still—O this is a selfish letter—I can make a living out of what is left; and it is the purest of all earthly affections; so even you must admit I think.

If either you or Kitty [Maxse] ever speak of my marriage again I shall write you such a lecture upon the carnal sins as will make you fall into each others arms; but you shall never come near me any more. Ever since Thoby died women have hinted at this, till I could almost turn against my own sex! But this will make no impression upon either of you.

   . . . Beloved Violet—you have a pure fount of sweet water in you—miraculous to me.

[336]   Yr. AVS

TO CLIVE BELL

[February 1907]   *46 Gordon Square, Bloomsbury*

My dear Clive,

   Your letter surely craves a premeditated answer; yet how did the correspondents of Gibbon achieve their share of the task? did they perambulate the study table too, casting periods as the angler casts his line or did they commend themselves to the sheet as simply as the child betakes itself to the Lords Prayer? I have a fancy that the great man was content with little eloquence in his friends if their attitude was pious.

   A true letter, so my theory runs, should be as a film of wax pressed close to the graving in the mind; but if I followed my own prescription this sheet would be scored with some very tortuous and angular incisions. Let me explain that I began some minutes since to review a novel and made its faults, by a process common among minds of a certain order or disorder, the text for a soliloquy upon many matters of importance; the sky and the breeze were part of my theme. A telegram however, with its necessary knock and its flagrant yellow, and its curt phrase of vicious English—I know not which sense was most offended—hit me in the wing and I fell a heaped corpse upon the earth. The sense, if that can be said to have sense which had so little sound, was to discredit the respectability of a house in Fitzroy Square. And there you see me in the mud. Shall I argue that a mind that knows not Gibbon knows not morality? or shall I affirm that bad English and respectability are twin sisters, dear to the telegram and odious to the artist? I state the question and leave it; for it will ramify if I mistake not through all the limbs of my soul and clasp the very Judgment seat of God. So then let us turn—and where? First, I think, to Vanessa; and I am almost inclined to let her name stand alone upon the page. It contains all the beauty of the sky, and the melancholy of the sea, and the laughter of the Dolphins in its circumference, first in the mystic Van, spread like a mirror of grey glass to Heaven. Next in the swishing tail of its successive esses, and finally in the grave pause and suspension of the ultimate A breathing peace like the respiration of Earth itself.

If I write of books you will understand that I continue the theme though in another key; for are not all Arts her tributaries, all sciences her continents and the globe itself but a painted ball in the enclosure of her arms? But you dwell in the Temple, and I am a worshipper without. It behoves me then to speak of common things, that are and cease to be; of people and of houses, of Empires and of governments.

I read then, and feel beauty swell like ripe fruit within my palm: I hear music woven from the azure skeins of air; and gazing into deep pools skimmed with the Italian veil I see youth and melancholy walking hand in hand. Yet why separate and distinguish when all are pressed to your ardent lips in one clear draught?

Let us then have make [sic] an ending: for in truth I must copy out this sheet.

[345]   Yours ever, AVS

The idea that Vanessa's name should stand alone upon a page was repeated in Virginia's dedication of her novel, Night and Day: 'To Vanessa Bell but, looking for a phrase, I found none to stand beside your name'.

IN THE SUMMER of 1907 Virginia and Adrian Stephen holidayed with Clive and Vanessa Bell at Rye. One of its residents was the American author Henry James, who had been a friend of Sir Leslie Stephen and was famous for his elaborate phrases and sentence construction.

TO VIOLET DICKINSON

Sunday [25 August 1907]   [The Steps, Playden, Sussex.]

My Violet,

    You drive me to write. O melancholy creature why do you see specialists? I wish to god you wouldnt. What you want, probably, is air and food and good society; here you should have a couch beneath an Apple tree, and sometimes I would sing to you, and sometimes I would leap from branch to branch, and sometimes I would recite, my own works, to the Zither.

    There comes a time, you see, when condolences are no use . . . all I can say is, why do you see doctors? They are a profoundly untrustworthy race; either they lie, or they mistake.

    Still, you will say, what the d—— does she know what it is to have a pain in the back—the worst thing about that little black devil is that she cant sympathise, once you get off her paper or her own spirits she feels nothing. Now, dirty devil (for your language is hot and strong—comes bubbling from the deep natural spring) amuse me. Well then, we went and had tea with Henry James today, and Mr and Mrs [George] Prothero, at the golf club; and Henry James fixed me with his staring blank eye—it is like a childs marble—and said "My dear Virginia, they tell me—they tell me—they tell me—that you—as indeed being your fathers daughter nay your grandfathers grandchild—the descendant I may say of a century—of a century—of quill pens and ink—ink—ink pots, yes, yes, yes, they tell me—ahm m m—that you, that you, that you *write in short*." This went on in the public street, while we all waited, as farmers wait for the hen to lay an egg—do they?—nervous, polite, and now on this foot now on that. I felt like a condemned person, who sees the knife drop and stick and drop again. Never did any woman hate 'writing' as much as I do. But when I am old and famous I shall discourse like Henry James. We had to stop periodically to let him shake himself free of the thing; he made phrases over the bread and butter 'rude and rapid' it was, and told us all the scandal of Rye. "Mr Jones has eloped, I regret to say, to Tasmania; leaving 12 little Jones, and a possible 13th to Mrs Jones; most regrettable, most unfortunate, and yet not wholly an action to which one has no private key of ones own so to speak.'' . . .

Nessa comes tomorrow—what one calls Nessa; but it means husband and baby, and of sister there is less than there used to be. But perhaps it is better; so the sanguine say. We are having Katharine Stephen for 2 nights, and then [Walter] Lamb and [Saxon] Sydney Turner; but I shall read and write, and only occasionally expose myself to their wisdom. I have 7 volumes of poetic drama to review for the Guardian, and a novel for the Times, and I want to write out many small chapters that form in my head; and to read Pindar, and a mass of other books; I know I shant. I begin to understand that I never shall. . . .

[380]   Yr. AVS

ABOVE: *Vanessa Bell with her elder son, Julian, at Studland Bay in 1910.*

To Clive Bell

Aug. 19th [1908]   *Sea View, Manorbier,* [*Pembrokeshire*]

My dear Clive,

There is no doubt but that I was well advised in telling you to come here for your honeymoon. I am surprised to find how beautiful it all is—more than I remembered—how lovely, and how primitive. I have not been on the cliffs yet, my business yesterday keeping me on the trot, but directly this letter is done, I am off to Proud Giltar.

Ah, it is the sea that does it! perpetual movement, and a border of mystery, solving the limits of fields, and silencing their prose. . . .

Well, what shall we discourse about? If I began upon literature, and slip by easy stages to a certain work; and I may as well ask you what you think of a Spanish name for the lady [Rachel Vinrace]. Cintra? Andalusia? Her father touched at many ports and sailors like sentimental names: he may have had other reasons too, not to be defined. . . .

I think a great deal of my future, and settle what book I am to write—how I shall re-form the novel and capture multitudes of things at present fugitive, enclose the whole, and shape infinite strange shapes. I take a good look at woods in the sunset, and fix men who are breaking stones with an intense gaze, meant to sever them from the past and the future—all these excitements last out my walk, but tomorrow I know, I shall be sitting down to the inanimate old phrases. . . .

[438]   Yr. AVS

Virginia was at work on her first novel, The Voyage Out, *originally entitled* Melymbrosia. *It was eventually published by Gerald Duckworth, Virginia's half-brother, in March 1915.*

TO CLIVE BELL

[23 January 1911]   *Bagley Wood, Oxford*

Dearest Clive,

 Tuesday would be best and, I need hardly say, delightful. On Friday I dont really get back till 5.30. Here I am in the heart (or perhaps that isnt the typical feature) of young womanhood. I like clever young women, in spite of my brother in law (That was said to tease).

 Gumbo [Marjorie Strachey, sister of Lytton] is seated at the piano, dressed in a tight green jersey, which makes her resemble the lean cat in the advertisement, singing O Dolche Amor, to her own accompaniment. The accompaniment ends: she flings her hands up, and gives vent to a passionate shriek; crashes her hands down again and goes on. A dry yellow skin has formed round her lips, owing to her having a fried egg for breakfast. Save that her songs are passionate, we have not mentioned the subject. But Roger [Fry] is discussed perpetually, and she has a letter from him, about her Friday club paper, which he takes to be a direct attack upon himself. Beginning my dear Marjorie: it ends Yrs. very sincerely. I have not seen her alone . . . . We had an icy motor drive over to Bagley. The motor broke down on the slope of a steep muddy hill; and Gumbo was seized with hysterics, imagining that a dog would run between her legs. I said that she need fear nothing of the kind, but did not give my reasons: and the baying of a hound in a far away farm made her fling herself upon Ray. Last night Gumbo gave us a long disquisition upon her character, talents,

ABOVE: *Saxon Sydney-Turner, Clive Bell, Virginia and Julian together on the beach at Studland Bay in 1910.*

LEFT: Lady Strachey, mother of Lytton, painted by Dora Carrington. It was owing to Lady Strachey's intervention that her nephew, Duncan Grant, was allowed to leave school and begin studying art.

LEFT: The Strachey Family, *a charcoal sketch by Duncan Grant, 1922.*

passions, and so forth; and told us that she would give all the praise she has for brilliance, if one person (preferably a man) would say she was lovely. No one rose. She has improved; and we get on better. No one makes me laugh more. She is a real figure.

Thus far I got; and then Ray's Miss Cox arrived. Miss Cox is one of the younger Newnhamites, and it is said that she will marry either a Keynes or a [Rupert] Brook. She has a superficial resemblance to a far younger and prettier Sheepshanks. She is a bright, intelligent, nice creature; who has, she says, very few emotions, but thinks so highly of Gwen [Darwin] that she even copies her way of speech. I am writing this in the waiting room at Oxford, having caught an unexpected omnibus on the high road, and thus arrived ½ an hour early. We played patience to an early hour this morning; and became very frank and indecent. Gumbo told us how her period affected her entrails, and finally destroyed her voice, upon which we all asked (she had been singing Brahms) whether she was now indisposed. It appeared that she was suffering from diarrhoea—all this pleased me very

much, and I repeat that I like clever young women. Also I had a compliment on my beauty. This was a little dashed by hearing that Gumbo had felt a distinct emotion of love upon last seeing Nessa.
[551]   Yrs. V.S.

Bagley was the home of Bertrand Russell. Ray (Costelloe) was the sister of Karin, who married Adrian Stephen. Katherine Cox ('Ka') studied at Newnham College, Cambridge, with Ray Costelloe, where she became a friend of Rupert Brooke. Virginia nicknamed her 'Bruin', suggesting loveable bear-like qualities. She was part of a group of friends at Cambridge who became known as the Neo-Pagans owing to their robust pursuit of the simple life.

TO CLIVE BELL

Saturday [March 1911]   Little Talland House, Firle

Dearest Clive,
  . . . I have just upon finished Desmonds Santayana, with amazement—whether at his powers or my own, or at the thoughts in the world, I cannot say. I think it is really astonishment at the number of disembodied things of great importance shut up in books. Having lived an active talkative life so long, prying into people through their sayings, I had rather forgotten how much thinking is done outside my own head. And yet, reading is like shutting the doors of a Cathedral, one becomes so pure. This would not apply to works of imagination, I suppose. Are you still a reader? . . .
[558]

Desmond MacCarthy had lent her a book by George Santayana.

IN MAY 1911 Virginia attended the marriage of the French painter, Jacques Raverat, to Gwen Darwin. The happiness they embodied left her aware of her own unmarried state. This contributed to the bout of

ABOVE: *Virginia with Rupert Brooke, Devon 1908. Rupert Brooke was a central figure in the Neo-Pagans. Whilst staying with Brooke at Grantchester, Virginia Woolf bathed naked with him by moonlight, although there was never, as this might imply, any romantic attachment between them.*

ABOVE: *Katherine Cox, painted by Duncan Grant. Familiarly known as 'Ka' and nicknamed 'Bruin' by Virginia, Katherine was another member of the Neo-Pagans. Virginia described her as a 'bright, intelligent, nice creature' but was also convinced that she had 'very few emotions'.*

depression she experienced the following month. However, this same month Leonard Woolf, another of Thoby Stephen's Cambridge friends, returned from Ceylon on leave, after an absence of nearly seven years. He had dined with the Stephens once in 1904, before leaving to take up employment in the Colonial Service in Ceylon. On meeting the Stephen sisters he had fallen in love with both simultaneously, but now that Vanessa was married he turned his attention to Virginia. Before his leave expired he had proposed marriage. Virginia did not immediately accept, but the remarkable honesty with which she responded to him gave him sufficient encouragement to resign from the Colonial Service. His gamble proved well advised: on 29 May 1912 Virginia agreed to marry him.

TO VANESSA BELL

Thursday [8? June 1911]   29 Fitzroy Square, W.

Beloved,

A dreadful Whitsunday blankness has descended upon us. We hoped that the storm would lighten the air—far from it. The storm was terrific. As nearly as possible Synge [Virginia] was taken from you. A great flash almost came in at the window. A church was set on fire.

Did you feel horribly depressed? I did. I could not write, and all the devils came out—hairy black ones. To be 29 and unmarried—to be a failure—childless—insane too, no writer. I went off to the Museum to try and subdue them, and having an ice afterwards, met Rupert Brooke, with, presumably, a Miss Olivier. Her beauty was marred by protruberant blemishes; as she wasn't beautiful, only a pretty chit, perhaps she wasn't Miss Olivier. . . .

[570]   Yr. B.

Miss Olivier refers to one of the four daughters of Sir Sydney Olivier, the Fabian Socialist—Margery, Brynhild, Daphne and Noel, all of whom were part of the Neo-Pagan group that centred around Rupert Brooke.

ABOVE: Jacques Raverat, *a woodcut by his wife, Gwen (née Darwin). Both had been Neo-Pagans. Virginia was extremely fond of them but nonetheless wrote dismissively to Vanessa about Gwen's work, though perhaps only to bolster her sister's confidence as an artist.*

ABOVE: Leonard Woolf, *by Duncan Grant, c. 1912, soon after his return on leave from Ceylon. Before their marriage Leonard shared Virginia and Adrian Stephen's house at 38 Brunswick Square, with Maynard Keynes as the other inhabitant. George Duckworth, in particular, found this disgracefully unconventional.*

TO LEONARD WOOLF

Saturday [13 January 1912]   *38 Brunswick Square*

My dear Leonard,

    I am rushing for a train so I can only send a line in answer [to your proposal]. There isn't anything really for me to say, except that I should like to go on as before; and that you should leave me free, and that I should be honest. As to faults, I expect mine are just as bad—less noble perhaps. But of course they are not really the question. I have decided to keep this completely secret, except for Vanessa; and I have made her promise not to tell Clive. I told Adrian that you had come up [from Frome where he was staying] about a job which was promised you. So keep this up if he asks.

    I am very sorry to be the cause of so much rush and worry. I am just off to Firle.

[600]   Yrs. VS

TO LEONARD WOOLF

May 1st [1912]   *Asheham* [Rodmell, Sussex]

Dearest Leonard,

    To deal with the facts first (my fingers are so cold I can hardly write) I shall be back about 7 tomorrow, so there will be time to discuss—but what does it mean? You can't take the leave, I suppose if you are going to resign certainly at the end of it. Anyhow, it shows what a career you're ruining!

    Well then, as to all the rest. It seems to me that I am giving you a great deal of pain—some in the most casual way—and therefore I ought to be as plain with you as I can, because half the time I suspect, you're in a fog which I don't see at all. Of course I can't explain what I feel—these are some of the things that strike me. The obvious advantages of marriage stand in my way. I say to myself. Anyhow, you'll be quite happy with him; and he will give you companionship, children, and a busy life—then I say By God, I will not look upon marriage as a profession. The only people who know of it, all think it suitable; and that makes me scrutinise my own

LEFT: Portrait of Virginia Woolf by Vanessa Bell, c. 1912. *Vanessa Bell painted a handful of portraits of her sister, some of which, though they omit facial detail, vividly convey the sitter's presence. Virginia was intrigued by her sister's Post-Impressionist style and her ability to suggest so much with so few means. This was one instance where painting was in advance of literature and it can be argued that the example of Post-Impressionism, with its reduction of detail and emphasis on form, inspired Virginia Woolf's re-shaping of the novel.*

ABOVE: *Virginia and Leonard, photographed at the time of their engagement. Virginia was to write to Jacques Raverat in 1922 that she 'couldn't have married anyone else'.*

motives all the more. Then, of course, I feel angry sometimes at the strength of your desire. Possibly, your being a Jew comes in also at this point. You seem so foreign. And then I am fearfully unstable. I pass from hot to cold in an instant, without any reason; except that I believe sheer physical effort and exhaustion influence me. All I can say is that in spite of these feelings which go chasing each other all day long when I am with you, there is some feeling which is permanent, and growing. You want to know of course whether it will ever make me marry you. How can I say? I think it will, because there seems no reason why it shouldn't—But I don't know what the future will bring. I'm half afraid of myself. I sometimes feel that no one ever has or ever can share something—Its the thing that makes you call me like a hill, or a rock. Again, I want everything—love, children, adventure, intimacy, work. (Can you make any sense of this ramble? I am putting down one thing after another). So I go from being half in love with you, and wanting you to be with me always, and knowing everything about me, to the extreme of wildness and aloofness. I sometimes think that if I married you, I could have everything—and then—is it the sexual side of it that comes between us? As I told you brutally the other day, I feel no physical attraction to you. There are moments—when you kissed me the other day was one—when I feel no more than a rock. And yet your caring for me as you do almost overwhelms me. It is so real, and so strange. Why should you? What am I really except a pleasant attractive creature? But its just because you care so much that I feel I've got to care before I marry you. I feel I must give you everything; and that if I can't, well, marriage would only be second-best for you as well as for me. If you can still go on, as before, letting me find my own way, as that is what would please me best; and then we must both take the risks. But you have made me very happy too. We both of us want a marriage that is a tremendous living thing, always alive, always hot, not dead and easy in parts as most marriages are. We ask a great deal of life, don't we? Perhaps we shall get it; then how splendid!

One doesn't get much said in a letter does one? I haven't touched upon the enormous variety of things that have been happening here—but they can wait.

D'you like this photograph?—rather too noble, I think. Here's another.
[615]   Yrs. VS

TO VIOLET DICKINSON

[4 June 1912]   38 Brunswick Square, W.C.

My Violet,

I've got a confession to make. I'm going to marry Leonard Wolf [sic].
He's a penniless Jew. I'm more happy than anyone ever said was
possible—but I insist upon your liking him too. May we both come on
Tuesday? Would you rather I come alone? He was a great friend of Thobys,
went out to India—came back last summer when I saw him and he's been
living here since the winter.

You have always been such a splendid and delightful creature, whom
I've loved ever since I was a mere chit, that I couldn't bear it if you
disapproved of my husband. We've been talking a great deal about you. I
tell him you [are] 6 ft 8: and that you love me.

My novels just upon finished. L. thinks my writing the best part of me.
We're going to work very hard. Is this too incoherent? The one thing that
must be made plain is my intense feeling of affection for you. How I've
bothered you—and what a lot you've always given me.
[620]   Yr. Sp.

ABOVE: *A photograph of Virginia found among her letters to Leonard written at the time of their engagement.*

THE HOGARTH PRESS

LEFT: Landscape at Asheham, by *Roger Fry*, c. 1912. *Asheham was a regular weekend and holiday retreat for Virginia and the other members of the Bloomsbury circle. This painting was owned by the Woolfs and still hangs at Monk's House.*

THE WOOLFS BEGAN their married life in a happy but unsettled state. They lived at three different addresses before finally, in 1915, taking Hogarth House, Richmond, all the while retaining the lease on Asheham, an isolated house in Sussex discovered by Virginia in 1911 and which they used for holidays and weekend retreats. Though unwell during much of the 1912–13 winter, Virginia completed her first novel, *The Voyage Out*, and submitted it in March 1913 to Duckworth's who published it two years later. In the summer of 1913 she fell seriously ill and, owing to the threat of insanity, was sent to a nursing home. Her condition remained serious throughout the rest of that summer. In consultation with doctors, Leonard reached the conclusion that it would be unwise for her to have children. 1914 was largely a year of recuperation.

Marriage to Leonard encouraged Virginia's literary aspirations. He, himself, published two novels and later became the literary editor of the *Nation*. He also devoted a large part of his life to politics, working with the Fabian Society and the Labour Party, and was to become a leading socialist authority on international affairs. He was exempted from military service, partly on medical grounds and partly because of his wife's unstable condition. He cared for Virginia devotedly and helped her through her most severe mental breakdown in the spring of 1915 when it was feared that her mind and character might be permanently impaired. Gradually she recovered and normal life returned.

At Hogarth House during 1916 Virginia began to conceive her second novel, *Night and Day*. She was at this stage leading a relatively quiet life, though their circle of friends and acquaintances was gradually expanding. As these letters reveal, her creativity fertilised her friendships, and friendships, in

ABOVE: Landscape with Haystack, Asheham, by *Vanessa Bell*, 1912.

THE HOGARTH PRESS

turn, stimulated her and fed her creativity. It is therefore not surprising that as her involvement with the art of novel-writing deepened, her social life became richer and more complex.

Another significant development in her life at this time was the decision with Leonard to set up the Hogarth Press. They produced their first publication in 1917, using a small printing press which was worked by hand. Leonard initially hoped that the manual labour which this venture involved would help rest Virginia's mind. But as the Press expanded into a flourishing business, it also deepened further her involvement with writers and writing.

Bloomsbury continued to provide her with an intimate core of friends. At the same time she began to enjoy friendships with certain literary figures, among them T. S. Eliot, Katherine Mansfield and John Middleton Murry. Another figure who sailed into view was the aristocrat Lady Ottoline Morrell whose character was as extravagant as her dress. Her homes, both in London and at Garsington in Oxfordshire, became meeting places for artists and writers, rivalling in attraction certain Bloomsbury haunts. Virginia, like other members of Bloomsbury, was intrigued by Lady Ottoline and by her court which included D. H. Lawrence, Aldous Huxley, the painter Mark Gertler and others. Another character who moves into focus is Dora Carrington, an ex-Slade student who rejected Gertler's love in favour of Lytton Strachey, with whom she set up a home, first at Tidmarsh, near Pangbourne, then at Ham Spray in Wiltshire. Her marriage to Ralph Partridge was in part to please Lytton who was in love with the younger man, and all lived together in a *ménage à trois*. Virginia observed with interest, affection and amusement the behaviour of Carrington and her friend from the Slade, Barbara Bagenal, and never let differences in age or temperament circumscribe her friendships. We find her at this period using letters to sustain and develop friendships, in this way creating around her a community of individuals that helped enrich her emotional and intellectual life.

THE HOGARTH PRESS

TO LYTTON STRACHEY

[early January 1915]   17 The Green, Richmond

Here is the book, which I hope will help the birth of many more
Victorian lives. I have seldom enjoyed myself more than I did last night,
reading Manning. In fact, I couldn't stop, and preserved some pages only
by force of will to read after dinner. It is quite superb—It is far the best
thing you have ever written, I believe—To begin with, what a miracle it is
that such a group should have existed—and then how divinely amusing
and exciting and alive you make it. I command you to complete a whole
series: you can't think how I enjoy your writing.
[718]   Yr. V.W.

*Strachey's essay on Cardinal Manning was the first of four essays which he published
as* Eminent Victorians *in 1918.*

TO LYTTON STRACHEY

28th Feb. [1916]   Hogarth [House], Richmond

Dearest Lytton,
    What a treat to hear from you!—still it doesn't make much difference
whether you write or not and I always feel you will turn up safe in the end,
and in fact you never really disappear . . . .
    Your praise [of *The Voyage Out*] is far the nicest of any I've had—having as
you know, an ancient reverence for your understanding of these things, so
that I can hardly believe that you *do* like that book. You almost give me
courage to read it, which I've not done since it was printed, and I wonder
how it would strike me now. I suspect your criticism about the failure of
conception is quite right. I think I had a conception, but I don't think it
made itself felt. What I wanted to do was to give the feeling of a vast tumult
of life, as various and disorderly as possible, which should be cut short for a
moment by the death, and go on again—and the whole was to have a sort

ABOVE: E.M. Forster, drawn by
William Rothenstein. *Virginia greatly
admired Forster's writing and felt he
understood her own work better than
anyone else. In 1925 she wrote to Gerald
Brenan, 'I always feel that nobody, except
perhaps Morgan Forster, lays hold of the
thing I have done.'*

of pattern, and be somehow controlled. The difficulty was to keep any sort of coherence,—also to give enough detail to make the characters interesting—which Forster says I didn't do. I really wanted three volumes. Do you think it is impossible to get this sort of effect in a novel;—is the result bound to be too scattered to be intelligible? I expect one may learn to get more control in time. One gets too much involved in details—But let us meet and have a long gossip . . .

[745]   Yr. V.W.

TO VANESSA BELL

April 26th [1917]   *Hogarth House, [Richmond]*

Dearest,

   . . . Our press arrived on Tuesday. We unpacked it with enormous excitement, finally with Nelly's help, carried it into the drawing room, set it on its stand—and discovered it was smashed in half! It is a great weight, and they never screwed it down; but the shop has probably got a spare part. Anyhow the arrangement of the type is such a business that we shant be ready to start printing directly. One has great blocks of type, which have to be divided into their separate letters, and founts, and then put into the right partitions. The work of ages, especially when you mix the h's with the ns, as I did yesterday. We get so absorbed we can't stop; I see that real printing will devour one's entire life. I am going to see Katherine Mansfield, to get a story from her, perhaps; please experiment with papers [for covers]. . . .

[829]   B.

TO VANESSA BELL

May 22nd [1917]   *Hogarth [House, Richmond]*

Dearest,

   We are coming to Asheham on Friday till Tuesday, so I hope we may meet. Perhaps you would say what suits you—We shall be alone. . . .
We've been so absorbed in printing that I am about as much of a farmyard sheep dog as you are. I can hardly tear myself away to go to London, or see

ABOVE: Lytton Strachey, by Duncan Grant, 1913. Strachey posed in the garden at Asheham and was painted not only by Grant but also by Roger Fry and Vanessa Bell, as a photograph of this occasion records.

ABOVE: Group at Asheham, by Duncan Grant, 1913. *The style of this painting reflects not only Grant's experiments with Post-Impressionist methods but also the relaxed informality that characterized Bloomsbury's weekend visits to this isolated house.*

anyone. We have just started printing Leonards story; I haven't produced mine yet, but there's nothing in writing compared with printing. . . .

However, I did rouse myself to go and see Ott. [Lady Ottoline Morrell]. I was so much overcome by her beauty that I really felt as if I'd suddenly got into the sea, and heard the mermaids fluting on their rocks. How it was done I cant think; but she had red-gold hair in masses, cheeks as soft as cushions with a lovely deep crimson on the crest of them, and a body shaped more after my notion of a mermaids than I've ever seen; not a wrinkle or blemish—swelling, but smooth.

Our conversation was rather on those lines, so I'm not surprised that I made a good impression. She didn't seem so much of a fool as I'd been led to think; she was quite shrewd, though vapid in the intervals. I begged her to revive Bedford Sqre and the salon, which she said she would, if anyone missed her. Then came protestations, invitations—in fact I dont see how we can get out of going there [Garsington], though Leonard says he wont, and I know it will be a disillusionment. However, my tack is to tell her she is nothing but an illusion, which is true, and then perhaps she'll live up to it. She was full of your praises. ''That exquisite head, on that lovely body—a Demeter—promising loaves and legs of mutton for us, and such sympathy, more feeling for others now. I did so enjoy my time at Wissett.'' . . . [837]   Yr. B

Leonard's story was 'Three Jews', and Virginia's, 'The Mark on the Wall'. Wissett Lodge in Suffolk had been rented in 1916 by Vanessa Bell in order that Duncan Grant and David Garnett might work on the attached land and thereby avoid conscription. Lady Ottoline had visited them there in August 1916.

ABOVE: Two woodcuts by Dora Carrington for 'Three Jews' by Leonard Woolf which, with 'The Mark on the Wall' by Virginia, comprises Two Stories, the first publication of the Hogarth Press in 1917.

ABOVE: A page from the 1927 edition of Kew Gardens (first published in 1919), in which Virginia's short story is decorated on every page by Vanessa Bell.

TO LADY OTTOLINE MORRELL

[May 1917]   Hogarth House, Paradise Road, Richmond

My dear Ottoline,

    . . . My images, after leaving you, were all of the depths of the sea—mermaid Queens, shells, the bones of the shipwrecked. I was incapacitated for normal life for some time after seeing you. It was a great pleasure, and reassurement to find that my memory had not been nearly mythical or romantic enough. But in what condition you are when the clock strikes 11 in the morning, I cant conceive—or how you order dinner;—or, in short, I shall follow you with my mouth agape. I've just sent you a halfpenny envelope containing a notice of our first publication. We find we have only 50 friends in the world—and most of them stingy. Could you think of any generous people—they need not be very generous —whose names you would send me? If so, I should be very grateful—

Your ever affate
Virginia Woolf.

[834]

TO ROGER FRY

Monday [18 November 1918]   Hogarth [House, Richmond]

My dear Roger,

I was just writing to insist upon being asked to dine with you, but was prevented by the fear that you might think it a bore. (I imagine you, quite honestly, having all sorts of people always about you, and rather liking to settle down alone occasionally). But there's nothing I should like better, and I only wish it happened oftener. What about next Friday, about 7.30, I suppose.

I think you *are* enviable, in spite of what you say, I dont mean so much in circumstances as in being yourself. I envy you for being that, but my envy is only skin deep, partly a measure of self-protection, and it doesn't interfere in the least with my profound affection. I'd much rather dine alone with you, and talk of innumerable things.

We've been having that strange young man Eliot to dinner. His sentences take such an enormous time to spread themselves out that we didn't get very far; but we did reach Ezra Pound and Wyndham Lewis, and how they were great geniuses, and so is Mr James Joyce—which I'm more prepared to agree to, but why has Eliot stuck in this mud? Can't his culture carry him through, or does culture land one there? Not that I've read more than

ABOVE: *Self-portrait by Roger Fry from his Twelve Original Woodcuts, published by the Hogarth Press in 1921.*

ABOVE: Lady Ottoline Morrell with T.S. Eliot at Garsington. In 1919 *Virginia wrote: 'On Saturday I go to Garsington; God knows why. Eliot is to be there.' Elsewhere she said that Garsington did not seem 'a house on the ground like other houses, but a caravan, a floating palace'.*

10 words by Ezra Pound by [sic] my conviction of his humbug is
unalterable. . . .

Yours ever

V.W.

[988]

*T. S. Eliot, now aged 30 and settled in England since 1905, had become Assistant
Editor of The Egoist in 1917. His first volume of poems, Prufrock, was published
the same year. At this dinner in Hogarth House, Eliot read to the Woolfs some of the
poems which they published in May 1919.*

TO KATHERINE ARNOLD-FORSTER

Aug. 12th [1919]   *Asheham, Rodmell, Lewes,* [Sussex]

Dearest Ka,

. . . We came down last month to look at the Round House; on the way
up from the station saw a notice of an old house to sell at Rodmell; went
and bought it at auction for £700; sold the Round House for £20 more than
we gave for it, and now in 10 days or so Mr Gunn is going to move us in
the farm waggons across the Bridge to Monk's House. That will be our
address for ever and ever; indeed I've already marked out our graves in the
yard which joins our meadow. . . .

Of course, literature is the only spiritual and humane career. Even
painting tends to dumbness, and music turns people erotic, whereas the
more you write the nicer you become. Do write the Life of somebody—a
vast fat book running over into the margins with reflections and cogitations
of all kinds. Do my dear Bruin—I assure you your style is perfectly fitted to
some rich thick compound, infinitely humane and judicious, not of course
to be run off in a hurry. But in the long winter evenings you might fill page
upon page.

Katherine Murry is, poor woman, very ill; she has been all the winter and
gets no better. Probably she will go to San Remo; but I feel rather dismal
about her. You thought her too painted and posed for your more spartan
taste I think. But she is all kinds of interesting things underneath, and has a

*RIGHT: Katherine Mansfield and
S.S. Koteliansky by Beatrice
Campbell. Virginia Woolf maintained an
uneasy relationship with Katherine
Mansfield, confiding in her diary after
Katherine's death: 'I was jealous of her
writing—the only writing I have ever
been jealous of . . . I have the feeling that
I shall think of her at intervals all
through life. Probably we had something
in common which I shall never find in
anyone else.' S.S. Koteliansky was a
Russian writer who, with Leonard
Woolf, translated the notebooks of
Chekhov.*

passion for writing, so that we hold religious meetings together praising Shakespeare. I dont much care for Murry's poems though. . . .

[1073]   Yr. V.W.

TO MARGARET LLEWELYN DAVIES

Sunday [16 November 1919]   Hogarth [House, Richmond]

Dearest Margaret,

I was extremely sorry not to see you yesterday . . . .

I dont really feel much difficulty in bearding you, all the same. You have an atmosphere; no doubt about that; but then all incorruptible and dominating characters have; and they suffer for their insight with one eye by being blind with t'other. I think thats the case with me too. We are imperfect human beings, but that's no obstacle to friendship, (on my side) in fact rather an incentive. You'll never like my books, but then shall I ever understand your Guild? Probably not.

As to Night and Day, and our argument, I was pleased to find on the hall table this testimony to my sympathy. I dont know that I agree, or with the other man who says I'm chiefly remarkable for common human wisdom? Massingham in the Nation this week is annoyed and abusive in a way that makes me feel I've done some good. Then there's the man who says I'm Jane Austen (but I'd much rather write about tea parties and snails than be Jane Austen). And a Bishop's wife detects undoubted Xtianity, and an elderly lady writes to tell me that the love scenes make her 'jumpy', but she feels that its, "the forerunner of a new species of book" (very intelligent). You see, its a question of the human heart, and cutting out the rotten parts according to ones convictions. Thats what I want to do, and thats where we differ, and thats why you'll dislike N. and D; and I shan't mind much if you do; but I should mind quite enormously if you didn't like me.

O yes, my dear Margaret, I think we've got a great deal in common; and you might ask me to dinner.

Your affate
Virginia

[1094]

THE HOGARTH PRESS

H. J. Massingham (1888–1952), editor of the Nation, regularly contributed articles on literary topics to the Nation and the Athenaeum.

KATHERINE MANSFIELD died on 12 January 1923, having been ill for some time with tuberculosis. She had spent the last years of her life in search of a cure and had settled for a while in Menton where she learnt that her husband, John Middleton Murry, had begun an affair with another writer. Virginia was both attracted and repelled by Katherine Mansfield, but in conversation with her touched on subjects she could share with few others. She watched her development as a writer jealously, recognizing her artistry but not always liking its effects.

TO DOROTHY BRETT

March 2nd [1923]   Hogarth House, Paradise Road, Richmond, Surrey

My dear Brett,

No you didn't tire me in the least—of course not. It was selfish of me, I felt, to make you talk about Katherine. I have wanted to so much since she died. But it must be very difficult for you. I've been looking in my diary and see that I must have written to her sometime in March 1921. From what you say, perhaps she never did get my letter. It makes me sorrier than ever that I did not simply persist—and yet I like to think that she had not, as I thought, taken some dislike to me, or got tired of hearing from me. I had been meeting [John Middleton] Murry, who was just going to join her, and he said she was lonely, and asked me to write. So I wrote at once, a very long letter, saying that she need only send one line, and I would go on regularly writing. It hurt me that she never answered, and then, as I was telling you, those gossips assured me that this was her game, and so on, and so on; until though I wanted to write, I felt that I no longer knew where we stood together, and so waited to see her—as I thought I certainly should.

I have been typing out letters this morning, and it is terrible to me to think that I sacrificed anything to their odious gossip. She gave me

ABOVE: *Aldous Huxley, Dorothy Brett and Mark Gertler at Garsington. Aldous Huxley was a regular visitor to Garsington and caricatured the life of the house and its hostess, Lady Ottoline Morrell, in his novel* Crome Yellow.

something no one else can. But here I am being selfish again. No one of my friends knew her, except you; and that is why I can't help going on to you. . . .

Ever yours
[1365]   V.W.

ABOVE: *Woodcut by Vanessa Bell, produced as an illustration to 'An Unwritten Novel', one of the short stories in* Virginia Woolf's Monday or Tuesday, *published by the Hogarth Press in 1921.*

VIRGINIA WOOLF turned forty in 1922 and entered upon her most fertile decade. Her first two novels, *The Voyage Out* (1915) and *Night and Day* (1919) had revealed unusual insights into the female mind, but while writing them she came to feel that the traditional format of the novel was cramping and inadequate. She experimented with a series of impressionistic sketches which she collected in the volume *Monday or Tuesday* (1921) and began to develop a stream-of-consciousness approach in her subsequent novel, *Jacob's Room* (1922). She aimed to promote a free-ranging narrative style, capable of reflecting the darting movement of the mind. In order for this method to result in coherence the novel had to be structured around something other than plot and character. In *Mrs Dalloway* (1925) the action is confined to the space of one day. In *To the Lighthouse* (1927) the novel falls into three sections which parallel the design of Lily Briscoe's painting, the completion of which brings the novel to a close. Virginia Woolf continued to experiment with the shape of the novel and in *The Waves* (1931) attempted to 'give the moment whole', in effect trying to write poetry in prose. These productive years also saw the appearance of *Orlando*, *A Room of One's Own* and *The Common Reader*, all of which helped establish her reputation as one of the most original authors of her day.

Fame extended the range of her social contacts. Somewhat warily she began to accept invitations from such society hostesses as Sybyl Colefax, Lady Cunard and Dorothy Wellesley. She was intrigued by the trappings of society, by its customs and love of display and by the personalities that composed it. But she was also aware that it promoted a more worldly set of values than those which concerned Bloomsbury. She was therefore careful to limit society's demands on her in order to

ABOVE: *The Novel, a woodcut by Roger Fry, taken from Twelve Original Woodcuts published by the Hogarth Press in 1921.*

protect that solitude necessary to a writer and so that she could continue her involvement with the Hogarth Press. Often her afternoons were spent setting type or wrapping up parcels of books alongside the other individuals whom she and Leonard had begun to employ as staff.

TO GERALD BRENAN

Christmas Day 1922   Monk's House, Rodmell, Near Lewes, Sussex

Dear Gerald,

Very stupidly I came away without your letter, though I have been putting off writing till Christmas, hoping to have time and some calmness. It interested me, very much, and now I can't take it up and answer it as I had meant. But no doubt this is as well. What one wants from a letter is not an answer. So I shall ramble on, until the cook goes off to tea with Mrs Dedman, when I must scramble the eggs.

First however, we certainly hope to come to you about the end of March, or beginning of April. This depends on things that can't be settled now; so may we leave it, and write definitely later? Apart from talking to you, as we want to do, at leisure, fully, at night, at dawn, about people, books, life, and so on and so on, my eyes are entirely grey with England—nothing but England for 10 years; and you can't imagine how much of a physical desire it becomes to feed them on colour and crags—something violent and broken and dry—not perpetually sloping and sloppy like the country here. (This is a very wet Christmas day).

I have been thinking a great deal about what you say of writing novels. One must renounce, you say. I can do better than write novels, you say. I don't altogether understand. I don't see how to write a book without people in it. Perhaps you mean that one ought not to attempt a 'view of life'?—One ought to limit oneself to one's own sensations—at a quartet for instance; one ought to be lyrical, descriptive: but not set people in motion,

ABOVE: London Garden, from Twelve Original Woodcuts by Roger Fry.

and attempt to enter them, and give them impact and volume? Ah, but I'm doomed! As a matter of fact, I think that we all are. It is not possible now, and never will be, to say I renounce. Nor would it be a good thing for literature were it possible. This generation must break its neck in order that the next may have smooth going. For I agree with you that nothing is going to be achieved by us. Fragments—paragraphs—a page perhaps: but no more. Joyce to me seems strewn with disaster. I can't even see, as you see, his triumphs. A gallant approach, that is all that is obvious to me: then the usual smash and splinters (I have only read him, partly, once). The human soul, it seems to me, orientates itself afresh every now and then. It is doing so now. No one can see it whole, therefore. The best of us catch a glimpse of a nose, a shoulder, something turning away, always in movement. Still, it seems better to me to catch this glimpse, than to sit down with Hugh Walpole, Wells, etc. etc. and make large oil paintings of fabulous fleshy monsters complete from top to toe. Of course, being under 30, this does not apply to you. To you, something more complete may be vouchsafed. If so, it will be partly because I, and some others, have made our attempts first. I have wandered from the point. Never mind. I am only scribbling, more to amuse myself than you, who may never read, or understand: for I am doubtful whether people, the best disposed towards each other, are capable of more than an intermittent signal as they forge past—a sentimental metaphor, leading obviously to ships, and night and storm and reefs and rocks, and the obscured, uncompassionate moon. I wish I had your letter for I could then go ahead; without so many jerks.

You said you were very wretched, didn't you? You described your liver rotting, and how you read all night, about the early fathers; and then walked, and saw the dawn. But were wretched, and tore up all you wrote, and felt you could never, never write—and compared this state of yours with mine, which you imagine to be secure, rooted, benevolent, industrious—you did not say dull—but somehow unattainable, and I daresay, unreal. But you must reflect that I am 40: further, every 10 years, at 20, again at 30, such agony of different sorts possessed me that not

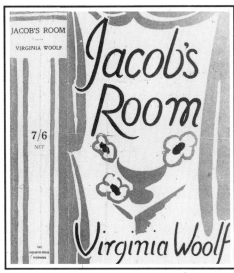

ABOVE: *Dust jacket to* Jacob's Room, *designed by Vanessa Bell and published by the Hogarth Press. Vanessa Bell's dust jackets, with their striking use of a few simple shapes, helped give to Hogarth Press publications a distinctive appearance.*

content with rambling and reading I did most emphatically attempt to end it all; and should have been often thankful, if by stepping on one flagstone rather than another I could have been annihilated where I stood. I say this partly in vanity that you may not think me insipid; partly as a token (one of those flying signals out of the night and so on) that so we live, all of us who feel and reflect, with recurring cataclysms of horror: starting up in the night in agony: Every ten years brings, I suppose, one of those private orientations which match the vast one which is, to my mind, general now in the race. I mean, life has to be sloughed: has to be faced: to be rejected; then accepted on new terms with rapture. And so on, and so on; til you are 40, when the only problem is how to grasp it tighter and tighter to you, so quick it seems to slip, and so infinitely desirable is it.

As for writing, at 30 I was still writing, reading; tearing up industriously. I had not published a word (save reviews). I despaired. Perhaps at that age one is really most a writer. Then one cannot write, not for lack of skill, but because the object is too near, too vast. I think perhaps it must recede before one can take a pen to it. At any rate, at 20, 30, 40, and I've no doubt 50, 60, and 70, that to me is the task; not particularly noble or heroic, as I see it in my own case, for all my inclinations are to write; but the object of adoration to me, when there comes along someone capable of achieving—if only the page or paragraph; for there are no teachers, saints, prophets, good people, but the artists—as you said—But the last sentence is hopelessly unintelligible. Indeed, I am getting to the end of my letter writing capacity. I have many more things to say; but they cower under their coverlets, and nothing remains but to stare at the fire, and finger some book till the ideas freshen within me, or they once more become impartible.

I think, too, there is a great deal of excitement and fun and pure pleasure and brilliance in one's fellow creatures. I'm not sure that you shouldn't desert your mountain, take your chance, and adventure with your human faculties—friendships, conversations, relations, the mere daily intercourse. Why do young men hold books up before their eyes so long? French literature falls like a blue tint over the landscape.

ABOVE: *Dust jacket to* The Common Reader, 1925, *by Vanessa Bell.*

LEFT: Portrait of Jacques
Raverat by Gwen Raverat.

But I am not saying what I mean, and had better stop. Only you must write to me again . . . And what about something for the Hogarth Press? . . .

Yours
Virginia Woolf

P.S.

I add a postscript, which is intended to explain why I say that one must not renounce. I think I mean that beauty, which you say I sometimes achieve, is only got by the failure to get it; by grinding all the flints together; by facing what must be humiliation—the things one can't do—To aim at beauty deliberately, without this apparently insensate struggle, would result, I think, in little daisies and forget-me-nots—simpering sweetnesses—true love knots—But I agree that one must (we, in our generation must) renounce finally the achievement of the greater beauty: the beauty which comes from completeness, in such books as War and Peace, and Stendhal I suppose, and some of Jane Austen; and Sterne; and I rather suspect in Proust, of whom I have only read one volume. Only now that I have written this, I doubt its truth. Are we not always hoping? and though we fail every time, surely we do not fail so completely as we should have failed if we were not in the beginning, prepared to attack the whole. One must renounce, when the book is finished; but not before it is begun. Excuse me for boring on: you may have said nothing of the kind. I was wondering to myself why it is that though I try sometimes to limit myself to the thing I do well, I am always drawn on and on, by human beings, I think, out of the little circle of safety, on and on, to the whirlpools; when I go under.
[1337]

TO JACQUES RAVERAT

July 30th 1923   *Hogarth House, Richmond*

My dear Jacques,

   I only got your letter two hours ago, on my English breakfast tray, with its bacon and egg: and I will answer at once. No, no, no. Nothing you said offended me: all delighted me; and I should have written ages ago if I had not always said "I'll write Jacques a nice long letter"—and so waited for the proper moment, and wrote meanwhile myriads of dreary drudgery. I find I never write to people I like. Jacques and Gwen require a good state of mind: whereas,—now you shall fill in the names of our old friends who can be put off with miserable relics.

We are all packed to go to Sussex tomorrow. This conveys nothing to you who have never seen the Hogarth Press. We travel with a selection of our books packed in hampers. Add to this a dog and a tortoise, bought for 2/- yesterday in the High Street. My husband presides with considerable mastery—poor devil, I make him pay for his unfortunate mistake in being born a Jew by discharging the whole business of life. This induces in me a sense of the transitoriness of existence, and the unreality of matter, which is highly congenial and comfortable. Now what do you think real? Gwen used to have views about that. Gwen was a highly dogmatic woman. Her breed is, alas, quite extinct. I assure you I can knock over the freeest thinker and boldest liver with the brush of a feather—nincompoop though I am, as far as logic goes.

This brings me, rather helter skelter, (but forgive thimble headedness in your old friend)—to the question of the religious revival: which concerns you both a good deal more nearly than you suspect. On my way back from Spain I stayed a week in Paris and there met Hope Mirrlees and Jane Harrison. This gallant old lady, very white, hoary, and sublime in a lace mantilla, took my fancy greatly; partly for her superb high thinking agnostic ways, partly for her appearance. "Alas," she said, "you and your sister and perhaps Lytton Strachey are the only ones of the younger generation I can respect. You alone carry on the traditions of our day." This referred to the miserable defection of Fredegond [Shove] (mass; confession; absolution, and the rest of it.) "There are thousands of Darwins" I said, to cheer her up. "Thousands of Darwins!" she shrieked, clasping her mittened hands, and raising her eyes to Heaven. "The Darwins are the blackest traitors of them all with that name!" she cried, "that inheritance! That magnificent record in the past!" "Surely", I cried, "our Gwen is secure?" "Our Gwen," she replied, "goes to Church, (if not mass, still Church) every Sunday of her life. Her marriage, of course, may have weakened her brain. Jacques is, unfortunately, French. A wave of Catholicism has invaded the young Frenchmen. Their children are baptised; their —'' Here I stopped her. ''Good God'', I said, ''I will never speak to them again! Whats more, I've just written a flippant, frivolous, atheistic letter to that very household, which will arrive precisely as the Host is elevated; they'll spit me from their lips, spurn me from their hearts—and, in short, religion has accomplished one more of her miracles, and destroyed a friendship which I'm sure began in our mother's wombs!'' All this eloquence left me dejected as a shovelful of cinders. Next week arrived your letter, which was the greatest relief in the world. Gwen is a militant atheist: the world renews itself: there is solid ground beneath my feet. I at once sent word to dear old Jane, who replied, a little inconsistently, ''Thank God''. . . .

I knew both the Murrys [John Middleton Murry and Katherine Mansfield]. Please read Katherine's works, and tell me your opinion. My theory is that while she possessed the most amazing *senses* of her generation so that she could actually reproduce this room for instance, with its fly, clock, dog, tortoise if need be, to the life, she was as weak as water, as insipid, and a great deal more commonplace, when she had to use her mind. That is, she can't put thoughts, or feelings, or subtleties of any kind into her characters, without at once becoming, where she's serious, hard, and where she's sympathetic, sentimental. Her first story which we printed, Prelude [1918], was pure observation and therefore exquisite. I could not read her latest. But prejudice may be at work here too. . . . [1414]   Ever Yrs. V.W.

ABOVE: John Middleton Murry, editor of the Nation and husband of Katherine Mansfield, photographed in 1935 by Howard Coster.

Katherine Mansfield's latest story, The Canary, had been published in the Nation in April 1923.

THE HOGARTH PRESS

TO ROGER FRY

Friday [24 August 1923]   *Monks House, Rodmell, [Sussex]*

My dear Roger,

I think your little book [*A Sampler of Castile*] is a perfect triumph. I don't deny that in parts the writing might be tightened with advantage, but as a whole it seems to me an amazing production, so subtle, so suggestive, so full of life, and sweeping together every kind of thing in such a way that it is perfectly easy to follow—I couldn't stop reading it. There's nothing quite like it that I know, and perhaps you've done nothing that so makes me stand in amazement at the sweep and range of your astonishing mind. I know you'll suspect me of flattery—but this is quite true—ask Clive if it isn't.

I think you would be very ill advised to leave out anything. The whole is so penetrated with interest of one kind or another that to break would merely be to mutilate. I have marked a very few slips which I have written on a sheet enclosed.

Indeed, I do think the Press is extremely lucky to get this book. You must go on and do more. I want to see you write about literature. I think you found a genuine and most successful way of giving shape to all sorts of things which normally run off in talk or thinking to oneself. And its odd and surprising to me how completely you have evolved your own language.

[1420]   Ever yr V.W.

MID-MARCH 1924, Leonard and Virginia moved out of Richmond and back to Bloomsbury, to 52 Tavistock Square where they were within easier reach of friends. At Virginia's request, Vanessa Bell and Duncan Grant executed decorations on the walls of the sitting-room. Whilst welcoming the increase in their social round which this move encouraged, Virginia also grew still fonder of their house at Rodmell, in Sussex, where she could retreat when in need of quietness and relative isolation.

LEFT: Virginia Woolf, 52 Tavistock Square, *watercolour by Vanessa Bell, c.* 1933–4 *and inscribed* 'V.B. to L.W., Christmas 1935'.

Jacques Raverat's illness now left him unable to write and he dictated his letters to Virginia to his wife, Gwen. Virginia, like other members of Bloomsbury at this time, was alarmed by the introduction into their circle of the ballet dancer, Lydia Lopokova, with whom Maynard Keynes was in love. Though an original and distinctive personality, she represented the shifting theatrical world and it was feared she would introduce a motley crew of foreigners and thereby alter the tone and ambience of Bloomsbury. The attitude of Virginia and Vanessa to Lydia was somewhat discreditable and it failed to dissuade Maynard. He married Lydia, after she had obtained a divorce from her first husband, and with her enjoyed much happiness.

TO JACQUES RAVERAT

June 8th 1924   Monks House, Rodmell, Lewes, [Sussex]

My dear Jacques,

I have left your last long and delicious letter—between you, you write damned good letters, whichever has the credit, the good Darwin or the bad Frog—in my box at home and so I can't answer your questions. What were they? . . . Two weeks ago I was in Cambridge, lecturing the Heretics upon Modern Fiction. Do you feel kindly towards Cambridge? It was, as Lytton would say, rather 'hectic'; young men going in for their triposes; flowering trees on the backs; canoes, fellows' gardens; wading in a slightly unreal beauty; dinners, teas, suppers; a sense, on my part, of extreme age, and tenderness and regret; and so on and so on. We had a good hard headed argument, and I respect the atmosphere, and I'm glad to be out of it. Maynard is very heavy and rather portentous; Maynard is passionately and pathetically in love, because he sees very well that he's dished if he marries her, and she has him by the snout. You can't argue solidly when Lydia's there, and as we set now to the decline, and prefer reason to any amount of high spirits, Lydia's pranks put us all on edge; and Bloomsbury steals off to its dens, leaving Maynard with Lydia on his knee, a sublime but heartrending spectacle.

ABOVE: Lady Ottoline Morrell, photographed by Cecil Beaton. Beaton's love of the theatrical well suited this naturally extravagant sitter.

LEFT: Horsechestnuts at Grantchester, *a woodcut by Gwen Raverat.*

Please do not repeat this gossip. Lydia came over here the other day and said "Please Leonard tell me about Mr Ramsay Macdonald. I am seerious—very seerious." However then she caught a frog and put it in an apple tree; and thats what so enchanting about her; but can one go through life catching frogs? You should hear Vanessa and Duncan on the subject.

I have had two bloody painful encounters with Middleton Murry; we stuck together at parties like two copulating dogs; but after the first ecstasy, it was boring, disillusioning, flat. The long and short of him is that he's a coward. First he fawns up to me, then when I attack him he plants his dart and runs away. He says we (Bloomsbury) deny our instincts: but why, after all, does writing badly prove that one is morally good? Answer me that, my dear Jacques: for I have no room to develop my own arguments. Now he's married a contributor to the Adelphi [Violet le Maistre] and is breeding.

Ottoline—was Ottoline ever a figure of any sort to you? She flaunts about London, not without a certain grandeur, as of a ship with its sails rat-eaten, and its masts mouldy, and green sea serpents on the decks. But no image will convey her mixture of humbleness and splendour and hypocrisy. She was shaking powder onto the floor and saying, "Virginia, why do women make up?"

We go back to London tomorrow. . . .

[1479]   Ever Yrs V.W.

THE MOST SIGNIFICANT new friendship that Virginia made during these years was with Vita Sackville-West whose beauty, aristocratic composure, daring and grasp of life she admired. With Vita she formed the deepest relationship outside her marriage and family. Though Virginia told another that Vita wrote with a pen of brass, she also admired her friend's 'rich dusky attic of a mind' and encouraged her to give her books to the Hogarth Press to publish.

Virginia had met Vita Sackville-West in 1922, but their friendship began slowly, with both seeming to want to test its basis. In the following letter Virginia is responding to Vita's taunt that she looked on everything, human relationships included, as mere copy, and that her approach to people was through the brain rather than the heart. Virginia's reply, though light and apparently offhand, opens the door to greater intimacy.

RIGHT: *Vita Sackville-West and her sons, Benedict (right) and Nigel (left). Virginia wrote of Vita: 'I like her & being with her; . . . There is her maturity & full breastedness: her being so much in full sail on the high tides, where I am coasting down backwaters; her capacity I mean to take the floor in any company, to represent her country . . . to control silver, servants, chow dogs; her motherhood . . . her being in short (what I have never been) a real woman.'*

TO V. SACKVILLE-WEST

19th August [1924]   Monk's House, Rodmell, Lewes, Sussex

My dear Vita,

Have you come back, and have you finished your book [*Seducers in Ecuador*]—when will you let us have it? Here I am, being a nuisance, with all these questions.

I enjoyed your intimate letter from the Dolomites. It gave me a great deal of pain—which is I've no doubt the first stage of intimacy—no friends, no heart, only an indifferent head. Never mind: I enjoyed your abuse very much.

LEFT: *T.S. Eliot and E.M. Forster at Monk's House. Virginia admired the work of both men, although she did describe Forster, in one letter to Vanessa, as 'limp and damp and milder than the breath of a cow'. In 1922 she was involved, with Lady Ottoline Morrell and others, in setting up an 'Eliot Fund' in an attempt to free Eliot from his job in a bank so that he could devote himself to writing. The project proved to be a source of considerable embarrassment to all concerned, Eliot eventually rejecting the financial aid offered him, and leaving the originators of the fund with the problem of what to do with the money collected.*

How could I think mountains and climbing romantic? Wasn't I brought up with alpenstocks in my nursery, and a raised map of the Alps, showing every peak my father had climbed? Of course, London and the marshes are the places I like best.

But I will not go on else I should write you a really intimate letter, and then you would dislike me, more, even more, than you do.

But please let me know about the book.

[1491]   Yr V.W.

BOTH VIRGINIA AND Leonard Woolf recognized T. S. Eliot, whom they first met in November 1918, as a supreme artist but they were sometimes irritated by his obsession with correct form, his inability to make up his mind and his excessive modesty. In the next letter Virginia teases these habits by picking up from a letter he had sent her his reference to himself as a 'Prince of Bores' and to his essays as 'defective compositions'. He had also written: 'Should I come to Eastbourne, we might visit you by dromedary for tea.'

TO T. S. ELIOT

3rd Sept. 1924   Monks House, Rodmell, Lewes, [Sussex]

My dear Tom,

It is a dreadful pity the Prince of Bores can't come to keep his reputation on the boil. Who knows? This time next year I may have found someone more princely and more boring, and where will you be then? However . . . Come by dromedary (this leaves me quite mystified) rather than not at all; and make Vivien come.

The serious answers to questions must now begin. We want your defective compositions as soon as we can have them. We should have them suitably printed, and produce after Christmas. Dont think that this allows you plenty of time; it does not. Send as soon as you have done your preface. I dont like paying fellow authors compliments, because I like there to be one cake of praise which is reserved entirely for me, but visiting Charleston the other day (my sister's) I there picked up The Sacred Wood and came home and burnt every one of my own leading articles in the [Times Literary] Supplement. Why are you the only man who ever says anything interesting about literature? There are we all pouring out gallons of ink weekly, and never a drop of it stays. However, I admire your work too much. It can't be as good as all that. But your brain seems to work.

Yes I am in the depth of modesty; cant bear my own writing; and wish I had been born with a gift for sewing instead.

But send us your manuscripts. The Criterion is praised on all sides. Clive, Mary etc etc.

[1495]   Yrs V.W.

The Criterion *was a magazine edited by Eliot.*

TO VITA SACKVILLE-WEST

Monday [15 September 1924]   Monk's House, Rodmell, Lewes, [Sussex]

My dear Vita,

I like your story [*Seducers in Ecuador*] very very much—in fact, I began reading it after you left, was interrupted by Clive, went out for a walk, thinking of it all the time, and came back and finished it, being full of a particular kind of interest which I daresay has something to do with its being the sort of thing I should like to write myself. I don't know whether this fact should make you discount my praises, but I'm certain that you have done something much more interesting (to me at least) than you've yet done. It is not, of course, altogether thrust through; I think it could be tightened up, and aimed straighter, but there is nothing to spoil it in this. I like its texture—the sense of all the fine things you have dropped in to it, so that it is full of beauty in itself when nothing is happening—nevertheless such interesting things do happen, so suddenly—barely too; and I like its obscurity so that we can play about with it—interpret it different ways, and the beauty and fantasticallity of the details—the butterflies and the negress, for instance. This is all quite sincere, though not well expressed.

I am very glad we are going to publish it, and extremely proud and indeed touched, with my childlike dazzled affection for you, that you should dedicate it to me. We sent to the printers this morning. . . .

I felt rather spirited up by your story, and wrote a lot—300 words—perhaps, this morning, and have a comfortable feeling that I am going to enjoy reading you again . . . By the way, you must let me have a list of people to send circulars to—as many as you can. And to do this you must come and see me in London for you should have heard Leonard and me sitting over our wood fire last night and saying what we don't generally say when our guests leave us, about the extreme niceness etc etc and (I'm now shy—and so will cease.)

[1497]   Yrs Ever V.W.

Vita had spent the night of 13 September with Virginia and Leonard, her first visit to Monk's House.

ABOVE: *Cushion cover designed by Duncan Grant for inclusion in the Lefèvre Gallery's Music Room, exhibited 1932.*

ABOVE: *Tile-topped table by Duncan Grant, decorated with a scene of Venus at her toilet. Signed and dated 1930.*

LEFT: Firescreen commissioned from Duncan Grant and stitched by his mother, Mrs Bartle Grant. It depicts a view from a window with a still life in the foreground. Mrs Grant learnt the technique of cross-stitch in order to execute her son's designs.

TO JACQUES RAVERAT

Oct. 3rd 1924   Monks House, Rodmell, [Sussex]

My dear Jacques,

    Certainly the painters have a great gift of expression. A highly intelligent account you seem to me to give of the processes of your own mind when I throw Neo Paganism in. In fact I rather think you've broached some of the problems of the writer's too, who are trying to catch and consolidate and consummate (whatever the word is for making literature) those splashes of yours; for the falsity of the past (by which I mean Bennett, Galsworthy and so on) is precisely I think that they adhere to a formal railway line of sentence, for its convenience, never reflecting that people don't and never did feel or think or dream for a second in that way; but all over the place, in your way.

    I'm writing now, partly because I was so much intrigued by your letter, and felt more in touch, partly because this is my last evening of peace. I go back to London tomorrow. Then there'll be people upon people; and I shall dash in and out, and go to concerts, and make engagements, and regret making engagements. The difficulty of writing letters is, for one thing, that one has to simplify so much, and hasn't the courage to dwell on the small catastrophes which are of such huge interest to oneself; and thus has to put on a kind of unreal personality; which, when I write to you for example, whom I've not seen these 11 years, becomes inevitably jocular. I suppose joviality is a convenient mask; and then, being a writer, masks irk me; I want, in my old age, to have done with all superfluities, and form words precisely on top of the waves of my mind—a formidable undertaking.

    About your letter, however; I didn't mean that private relations bore me: which is indeed an intolerable perversion of my real meaning, who find relations of all kinds more and more engrossing, and (in spite of being made a fool of so often by one's impulse to surrender everything—dignity and propriety—to intimacy) final, in some way; enduring: gigantic; and beautiful. Indeed, I find all this in my relations with people, and what I can guess of theirs. What I meant was that *sexual* relations bore me more than they used: am I a prude? Am I feminine? Anyhow for two years past, I have been a spectator of I daresay a dozen affairs of the heart—violent and crucial; and come to the conclusion that love is a disease; a frenzy; an epidemic; oh but how dull, how monotonous, and reducing its young men and women to what abysses of mediocrity! Its true that all my lovers were of the simplest type; and could only flush and fade crudely like sea anemones bathed now blue, now red. Thats what I meant, I think.

Our loves, yours and mine and that granite monolithic Gwens—(until she writes to me, I shall say what I like in abuse of her to her husband) were of a very different kind. But then we were creatures of temperament. No: your admiration of me was not apparent; but then I was alarmed of your big nose, your bright eyes, your talking French, and your having such a quick easy way with you, as if you had solved the problems of life,—gone straight into the middle of the honeycomb without one miss. Yes—thats how I figure you: thats still (vaguely now) the image I have of my dear and adorable Jacques—but I should never have dared call him so to his face. And then, (this is a secret) for some reason, your and Gwen's engagement, being in love, took on for me a symbolical character; which I even tried to put down in writing. All very absurd I suppose: still you were very much in love, and it had an ecstatic quality. Indeed, you will laugh, but I used to think of you, in a purely literary way, as the two people who represented that passion in my mind: and still, when I think of you, I take out my brush, and paint both of your faces a divine sunset red. How oddly composed are one's feelings! You would never have guessed, I daresay, that Jacques and Gwen always appear to Virginia in a sunset glow?

As for gossip, I hope to collect some in the great world.

Vanessa is getting a little querulous about Maynard and Lydia, and will have, she says, to turn out. Our Mrs Joad has left her Mr Joad. Our Dadie [George Rylands] is a very nice boy. Our Karin Stephen sent me to bed with a violent headache last week, and ruined the last page of my novel (Oh yes, I'll write another letter and tell you about my writing—anything you want to know). She descended on us, and God knows I like her; but there's a deafness of the spirit about her, which exhausts more than dragging a ton of coal upstairs. So hearty she is, good humoured, and right minded. The poor devil interests me for having tried to live with Adrian, and for being

ABOVE: Photograph of Gwen Raverat, née Darwin.

ABOVE: Lydia Lopokova, photographed by Cecil Beaton. Lydia was a principal dancer in Diaghilev's company; Maynard Keynes fell in love with her in 1922.

LEFT: Baron and Baroness Keynes, by *William Roberts, 1932. The relationship between Maynard and Lydia initially dismayed Bloomsbury. In 1922 Virginia wrote to Vanessa: 'I can forsee only too well Lydia stout, charming, exacting; Maynard in the Cabinet; 46 Gordon Square the resort of the dukes and prime ministers. M. being a simple man, not analytic as we are, would sink beyond recall long before he realized his state. Then he would awake, to find 3 children, and his life entirely and for ever controlled.' Despite these ominous predictions, the couple had a happy and successful marriage.*

inarticulately aware of her own obtuseness. She can't feel; she cant enjoy; she cant be intimate: she cares for nothing. Yet she has the most perfect apparatus for life in body and head and wealth and freedom. To cure herself she pays £1 daily to a psychoanalyst; and would, she told me, prefer to be entirely destitute could she only feel things, instead of being as she is now non-feeling. But this may convey nothing to you.

However, I'm awfully shy of saying how really and truly I would do a great deal to please you and can only very very dimly murmur a kind of faint sympathy and love.

[1501]   Yrs V.W.

Mrs Joad was an employee with the Hogarth Press. Karin Stephen (née Costelloe) had married Virginia's brother Adrian during the First World War. She suffered from deafness, a disability that did not prevent her eventually becoming a psychoanalyst.

JACQUES RAVERAT'S ILLNESS was getting steadily worse. Aware of this, he began composing his autobiography which he never completed.

TO JACQUES RAVERAT

Nov 29th 1924   Tavistock Square, W.C.I

My dear Jacques,

I am much distressed, not figuratively but genuinely, to hear what a horror of a time you have been having. It was tantalising to see old Gwen for such a second, but the best of these Darwins is that they are cut out of the rock, and three taps is enough to convince one how immense is their solidity (to which Gwen has added, I thought, some vein of wisdom, and sweetness of temper which I rather envy her—I like seeing women weather the world so well). . . .

One reflection occurred to me, dealing with our Mrs Joad . . . how much nicer young women are than young men. I hope to get a rise out of you. Nicer, I say, humaner, less conceited, more sensitive, —not cleverer. . . .

THE HOGARTH PRESS

Now please tell me about your autobiography, which so whets my curiosity that I must entreat you to let me see it. If I translated it, couldn't we publish it?

Please write it with a view to this, and let it be the waste paper basket, conduit pipe, cesspool, treasure house, and larder and pantry and drawing and dining bed room of your existence. Write about everything, without order, or care. Being a Frog, you won't of course: you will organise and compose. Still, let me see it, and get on with it.

It is awful how business runs away with one's time. Soon I shall have to describe a fresh set of people to you—a man called Angus Davidson, who thinks of coming to us [the Hogarth Press]. Then, socially, what about Lady Colefax? Being the most successful, hardest mouthed hostess in London, she retains spots about the size of a sixpenny piece of astonishing sensibility on her person. Having left her umbrella here, I, in malice or sport, proceeded to describe it, glowing and gleaming among my old gamps. Whereupon this hard bitten old hostess of 50 flushed quite red, and said "Mrs Woolf, I know what you think of my umbrella—a cheap, stubby, vulgar umbrella, you think my umbrella: and you think I have a bag like it—a cheap flashy bag covered with bad embroidery". And it was too true. Only, if she saw it, must there not be depths in Lady Colefax? Think this out, and let me know.

Please write and say how you are.

[1515]   Yrs V.W.

TO JACQUES RAVERAT

Dec. 26th 1924   Monk's House, Rodmell, [Sussex]

My dear Jacques,

Do not expect wit or sense in this letter, only the affection of a drugged and torpid mind. Oh an English Christmas! We are not Christians; we are not social; we have no part in the fabric of the world, but all the same, Christmas flattens us out like a steam roller; turkey, pudding, tips, waits, holly, good wishes, presents, sweets; so here we sit, on Boxing day, at Rodmell, over a wood fire, and I can only rouse myself by thinking of you. In particular, I want to know 1. how you are. 2. Whether you are getting on with your autobiography; 3. What you are thinking; 4. what feeling; 5. what imagining, criticising, seeing—do catch that wild woman Gwen and stick a pen in her paw.

All that I predicted about Maynard and Lydia is coming to pass. They dined with us 2 nights ago: and my God! the poor sparrow is already turning into a discreet, silent, serious, motherly, respectable, fowl, with eggs, feathers, cluck cluck clucking all complete. A melancholy sight indeed, and I foresee the day when she dislikes any reference to dancing. Maynard is—But enough of the Keynes', as they are called in Bloomsbury. "Mr Keynes has very bad taste," my cook said to me, after the dinner. "Madame laughs, and he is so serious". Soon Vanessa is escorting her to the divorce court. Once divorced, she will give up dancing. But enough of the Keynes.

Now who shall we pitch on? Casting a shadow over my paper at the present moment, is the fine oriental head of Angus Davidson. He is staying here to know us and be known (he is our partner now) and, despite his

ABOVE: The Raverat household and friends in the south of France.

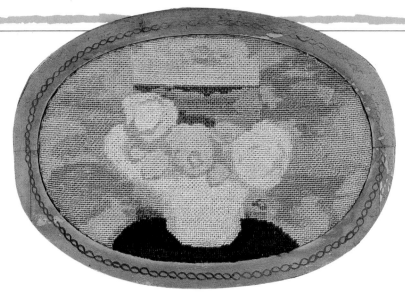

brother's [Douglas] neck, I like him very much; and think him likely to be our salvation—gentle, considerate, cautious, kind, with a mind smooth and sensitive as the thickest cream. Do you know that quality in young well-bred Englishmen? Slightly hesitating, diffident, and unselfconscious. He is working in cross stitch at a design by Duncan for a chair; Leonard is ordering onions from a catalogue. . . .

Who is there next? Well, only a high aristocrat called Vita Sackville-West, daughter of Lord Sackville, daughter of Knole, wife of Harold Nicolson, and novelist, but her real claim to consideration, is, if I may be so coarse, her legs. Oh they are exquisite—running like slender pillars up into her trunk, which is that of a breastless cuirassier (yet she has 2 children) but all about her is virginal, savage, patrician; and why she writes, which she does with complete competency, and a pen of brass, is a puzzle to me. If I were she, I should merely stride, with 11 Elk hounds, behind me, through my ancestral woods. She descends from Dorset, Buckingham, Sir Philip Sidney, and the whole of English history, which she keeps, stretched in coffins, one after another, from 1300 to the present day, under her dining room floor. But you, poor Frog, care nothing for all this.

Roger Fry is getting a little grumpy. He is not, you see, (or I imagine you see) a born painter, and this impediment seems to obstruct the run of his

LEFT: Lady Seated in an Omega Interior, *Roger Fry. The Omega Workshops were the inspiration of Roger Fry who wanted to see a Post-Impressionist use of colour and shape spill over into the applied arts. To this end he employed artists to decorate furniture and to design fabrics and rugs. His fellow directors were Vanessa Bell and Duncan Grant. The Omega ran from 1913 until 1919. Virginia Woolf patronized it to an extent but balked at buying an Omega dress. 'My God! What colours you are responsible for!' she wrote to Vanessa. 'Karin's [Adrian Stephen's wife] clothes almost wrenched my eyes from the sockets—a skirt barred with reds and yellows of the vilest kind, and a pea green blouse on top, with a gaudy handkerchief on her head, supposed to be the very boldest taste. I shall retire into dove colour and old lavendar, with a lace collar, and lawn wristlets.'*

sympathies, so that he makes no allowances, but judges the imperfect and frail purely as if he were still an impeccable undergraduate, an incorruptible Apostle: whereas for my part I grow more mellow every day.

There!

I think I will leave off with that tribute to myself.

Love from everybody in the room.

[1520] Yours aff. V.W.

Lydia Lopokova was separated from her first husband. She married Maynard Keynes in 1925. Angus Davidson, a young man with a rather sleepy temperament who came to work for the Hogarth Press, was a friend of Duncan Grant and the brother of the painter, Douglas Davidson.

TO JACQUES RAVERAT

Feb: 5th 1925 52 Tavistock Square, [W.C.1]

My dear Jacques,

I was struck down with influenza the very day I wrote to you, and am still in bed. Otherwise, I should have sent off my proofs [of *Mrs Dalloway*] before, but they were muddled up, and influenza makes me like a wet dish cloth—even to sort them was beyond me. I have left them uncorrected. Much has been re-written. Do a little re-writing on my behalf. Anyhow, don't cast me from you; and say nothing, or anything, as you like. (It will be sent tomorrow, 6th.).

Being bedridden, my view of the world has had a great thumb put over it. I can't think how you keep so sharp and clear. I have seen Clive Bell, who gave me another headache; he is a good fellow, however. I was so rash as to tell him he praised his Polly Flinders too much—his pretty Poll—his paramour—his Mary Hutch [Hutchinson] I mean. (I forgot if you are aware of that highly respectable alliance, which is far more lasting and punctiliously observed than any marriage). I said he should not be praising her legs in company, or cracking up her little witticisms, or even repeating the tributes of other gentlemen. But, he said, he did it to show Vanessa that she is a serious human being. He said, just because Mary dresses well, and

ABOVE: Vanessa Bell. *Pen and ink sketch by Duncan Grant, 1920.*

ABOVE: The Bell Children, *a drawing by Duncan Grant.*

you and Nessa badly, you think her dull: so I must prove how silly you both are.

Clive is now shaped like a spade and thick as an oak tree. He wears bright blue socks, which he is forever hitching up, and his trousers, for some reason which a man may know, are always above his knees. But how good hearted he is—bunches of grapes arrive for me; and yet I never do anything but bite his nose off when I see him, and laugh at him behind his back. I have an idea you and Gwen hated him. Let me assure you, you were wrong. Not that I claim for him any of the heroic virtues. Being bred a Puritan, (in the main—but I had a French great grandmother to muddle me) I warm my hands at these red-hot-coal men. I often wish I had married a foxhunter. It is partly the desire to share in life somehow, which is denied to us writers. Is it to you painters? Ever since I was a child I have envied people who did things—but even influenza shall not mislead me into egoistical autobiographical revelations . . . Of course, I long to talk to you about myself, my character, my writings, but am withheld—by what?

Karins party came off last night, and I lay in bed and imagined it all very brilliant. Leonard put on his deceased brother-in-law's (who died in a Bath at Eastbourne) dress clothes, and went off to brew the punch. Hope Mirrlees arrived half an hour early (do you admire her novels?—I can't get an ounce of joy from them, but we like seeing her and Jane [Harrison] billing and cooing together). Then came 40 young Oxford men, and three very pretty girls; Vanessa, Mary Hutch, Clive and Lytton—Lytton gravitated to the 40 young men, and was heard booming and humming from flower to flower. Vanessa, who had not dressed, sat commandingly on a sofa, talking to a sculptor called Tomlin, and to no one else, for she is beyond the pale now, makes no attempt to conciliate society, and often shocks me by her complete indifference to all my floating loves and jealousies, but with such a life, packed like a cabinet of drawers, Duncan, children, painting, Roger—how can she budge an inch or find a cranny of room for anyone? Clive came in late, having been dining with Mary at her new house in Regent's Park. She has a ship's steward to serve at table, and whether for this reason or another provides the most spicy liquors, foods, cocktails and

ABOVE: Mary Hutchinson, watercolour by Duncan Grant, 1915. Mary had a long-standing affair with Clive Bell from 1918 to 1927. Clive went to great pains to convince his friends that she was a serious, intelligent woman. Virginia once described Mary as 'mute as a trout—I say trout because of her spotted dress—also because, though silent, she has the swift composure of a fish.'

so on—for example an enormous earthenware dish, last time I was there, garnished with every vegetable, in January—peas, greens, mushrooms, potatoes; and in the middle the tenderest cutlets, all brewed in a sweet stinging aphrodisiac sauce. I tell you, I could hardly waddle home, or compose my sentiments. So Clive gets a little warm, and very red about the gills towards midnight.

Then Karin, who felt the approach of disillusionment about eleven, ran down to the kitchen and borrowed the housemaid's gramophone. The 40 young men began waltzing, and the three lovely girls sat together flirting in corners. Isn't it an odd thing that Bloomsbury parties are always thus composed—40 young men; all from Oxford too, and three girls, who are admitted on condition that they either dress exquisitely, or are some man's mistress, or love each other. Much preferring my own sex, as I do, or at any rate, finding the monotony of young mens' conversation considerable, and resenting the eternal pressure which they put, if you're a woman, on one string, find the disproportion excessive, and intend to cultivate women's society entirely in future. Men are all in the light always: with women you swim at once into the silent dusk. But to return. They danced. Leonard got horribly bored. He was set upon by little Eddie Sackville West, who is as appealing as a kitten, a stray, a mangy, unloved kitten; and this poor boy, after pouring forth his woes (all men confide in Leonard—especially such as love their own sex) sat by mistake down on the best tea cups. Being an aristocrat out of his element, he was considerably discomposed. Sweets and jams stuck to his behind, and Leonard had to dust him, and pat him, and finally leave him; trying I believe, to smoke a pipe in full evening dress, and white waistcoat. They work very hard, the aristocracy. Karin was heard to say, between the waltzes, Isn't this jolly?—On being assured it was, she plucked up heart, and means to give another party, with another hostess, next month.

Really, you have done me good. This is the first time I have cantered out on paper this fortnight. I find a great pleasure in waking all the doves in their dovecots—in stirring my words again. But this I can never explain to a painter, I suppose; how words live in companies, never used, except when one writes.

ABOVE: Mary Hutchinson, by *Vanessa Bell, 1915, a copy of a painting now in the Tate Gallery in London.*

RIGHT: The Hammock, by Duncan Grant, 1921–3. *Vanessa reclines in the hammock which is rocked by Quentin, whilst Angelica walks down the path. Julian is shown in a boat on the pond. The seated figure reading is presumably Duncan himself. Various studies for this picture suggest that Duncan Grant intended it as a formal celebration of the idyll that Charleston represented.*

What about the autobiography? You jeered at me for saying I would print it. But I swear I will. I can see the very book it shall be and if you don't look out, I shall add to it some of your pictures, with a description of them from my own pen. (This is a threat, because writers can't write about anything except writing).

So now I must stop, and do a little cross stitch, and I shall dwell upon you, as indeed I have been doing a great deal, lying here—and though you'll snap my nose off for saying so—with considerable admiration as well as affection.

[1534]   Yours V.W.

Clive Bell was a great admirer of the female sex but the woman who remained the longest in his company was Mary Hutchinson. Aware that Bloomsbury devalued her, Clive had developed the habit of over-praising her in their company. Stephen Tomlin, the sculptor (then aged 24), later made bust portraits of Virginia Woolf and Lytton Strachey and, after an affair with Duncan Grant, married Julia Strachey. Eddie Sackville-West, a cousin of Vita, became heir to Knole. A novelist, critic and brilliant painter, he translated Rilke and was one of the first to recognize the greatness of Kafka. His life was dogged by ill health and unhappy personal relationships.

ABOVE: The sitter in this portrait drawing by Duncan Grant and dated 1930 is thought to be the sculptor Stephen Tomlin. Virginia first met Tomlin in December 1924 and recorded in her diary, 'There's a little thrush-like creature called Tomlin who wants to sculpt me'. She did not sit for him until the summer of 1931; the resulting bust can now be seen in the National Gallery, London.

ON 7 MARCH 1925 Jacques Raverat died. Shortly before then he had received the proofs of *Mrs Dalloway* which Virginia had sent him. After reading them he had dictated a letter to Virginia which, as she explained to his wife Gwen, gave her great happiness.

TO GWEN RAVERAT

11th March [1925]   52 Tavistock Square, W.C.1

Dearest Gwen,

Your and Jacques' letter came yesterday, and I go about thinking of you both in starts, and almost constantly underneath everything, and I don't know what to say. The thing that comes over and over is the strange wish I have to go on telling Jacques things. This is for Jacques, I say to myself; I want to write to him about happiness, about Rupert [Brooke], and love. It had become to me a sort of private life, and I believe I told him more than anyone, except Leonard; I become mystical as I grow older and feel an alliance with you and Jacques which is eternal, not interrupted, or hurt by never meeting. Then of course, I have now for you—how can I put it?—I mean the feeling that one must reverence?—is that the word—feel shy of, so tremendous an experience; for I cannot conceive what you have suffered. It seems to me that if we met, one would have to chatter about every sort of little trifle, because there is nothing to be said.

And then, being, as you know, so fundamentally an optimist, I want to make you enjoy life. Forgive me, for writing what comes into my head. I think I feel that I would give a great deal to share with you the daily happiness. But you know that if there is anything I could ever give you, I would give it, but perhaps the only thing to give is to be oneself with people. One could say anything to Jacques. And that will always be the same with you and me. But oh, dearest Gwen, to think of you is making me cry—why should you and Jacques have had to go through this? As I told him, it is your love that has forever been love to me—all those years ago, when you used to come to Fitzroy Square, I was so angry and you were so furious, and Jacques wrote me a sensible manly letter, which I answered, sitting at my table in the window. Perhaps I was frightfully jealous of you both, being at war with the whole world at the moment. Still, the vision has become to me a source of wonder—the vision of your face; which if I were painting I should cover with flames, and put you on a hill top. Then, I don't think you would believe how it moves me that you and Jacques should have been reading Mrs Dalloway, and liking it. I'm awfully vain I know; and I was on pins and needles about sending it to Jacques; and now I feel exquisitely relieved; not flattered: but one does want that side of one to be acceptable —I was going to have written to Jacques about his children, and about my having none—I mean, these efforts of mine to communicate with people are partly childlessness, and the horror that sometimes overcomes me.

ABOVE: Gwen Raverat with one of her children.

ABOVE: Rupert Brooke, a woodcut portrait by Gwen Raverat, the frontispiece to his Collected Poems. After Brooke's death Virginia wrote to Ka Cox: 'I never think his poetry good enough for him, but I did admire him very much indeed, and he always seemed to me like a fully grown person among mummies and starvelings . . .

There is very little use in writing this. One feels so ignorant, so trivial, and like a child, just teasing you. But it is only that one keeps thinking of you, with a sort of reverence, and of that adorable man, whom I loved.

[1541]   Yours V.W.

TO GWEN RAVERAT

April 8th 1925   *52 Tavistock Sqre.*

Dearest Gwen,

    After all, we had to come back a day earlier than we meant, as the hotel became crowded. But we had snuffed up every moment—it was fine incessantly, and I now see why you and Jacques pitched on the borders of that sea. But I was going, inconsistently, to beg you to live in London. Trust me to find you a house. Then I would flirt with your daughters, and talk the sun out of the sky with you. Paris is a hostile brilliant alien city. Nancy Cunard and Hope Mirrlees and myriads of the ineffective English live there, or rather hop from rock to rock. Here we grow slowly and sedately in our own soil. Coming back last night was like stepping into some grave twilit room, very spacious and quiet, with a few lights and the great misty squares, and everything very mute and muffled, and out at elbows.

    I cannot think what I was going to write to Jacques about love. I constantly thought of him lying among those terraces and vineyards, where it is all so clear cut, and logical and intense, and it struck me that, from not having seen him all these years, I have no difficulty in thinking him still alive. That is what I should like for myself, that there should be no breach, no submission to death, but merely a break in the talk. I liked that uncompromising reality of him: no sentimentality, and no beating about the bush. This is all very ill written, chopped and jerky, when I should like to write even the racketiest letter to Gwen beautifully, but I went out early this morning to see Nessa's new house [37 Gordon Square], and saw a woman killed by a motor car. This pitches one at once into a region where there is no certainty and one feels somehow, abject and cowed—exalted. I want so much to understand my own feelings about everything, to unravel

THE HOGARTH PRESS

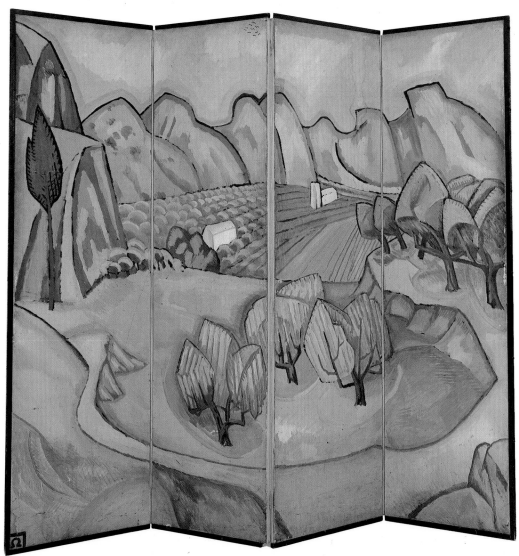

LEFT: View of a Provençal Valley, a screen produced by Roger Fry for sale at the Omega. Fry's choice of subject reflects his great love of the south of France. He regularly visited Provence in order to paint and towards the end of his life bought a farmhouse at St Rémy de Provence.

THE HOGARTH PRESS

LEFT: Jeu de Boules, Vence in Sunlight, *woodcut by Gwen Raverat, 1925.*

RIGHT: *Vita Sackville-West, in 1924. The friendship between Vita and Virginia was beginning to turn into something much more intense. Virginia described Vita as being '. . . like an overripe grape in features, moustached, pouting, will be a little heavy; meanwhile, she strides on fine legs, in a well cut skirt . . . Oh yes, I like her; could tack her on to my equipage for all time; & suppose if life allowed, this might be a friendship of a sort.'*

and re-christen and not go dreaming my time away. Jacques' death will probably make you, because it will so intensify everything, a very interesting woman to me. But as I said before, I cannot conceive such an experience, not at your age. . . .

This morning to hearten myself, I read Jacques letter about Mrs Dalloway again. I was afraid and indeed half sure, he wouldn't like it, as I meant to have asked him to let me dedicate to him. When you have time one day, do tell me why you liked it—or anything about it. This is partly author's vanity and that consuming interest in one's own work which is not entirely vanity—partly it springs from my own feeling that to be brought before you and Jacques was a tremendous ordeal, at that time, and the impression it made on you would mean more to me than what other people could say of it. But forgive this importunity, I am off for Easter to Rodmell—a place you'll have to visit. But when are you coming over? I can't tell you how that 10 days at Cassis has burnt truly upon my mind's eye the beauty and our happiness, and you and Jacques. Well, I am interrupted by an author, who rings up and says he or she must deliver a manuscript into my own hands. What about Jacques' autobiography?

This is a scrap—but only in meaning, for it is too long. I am too harried to write a nice letter, and yet I don't think you mind whether one writes a nice letter or not, so I shall send it. And I will certainly keep up the habit of garrulity, to which Jacques induced me. I never write a word to anybody nowadays—except for him, I don't think I wrote a letter in 8 weeks.

Tell me about your children.

Does the little creature [Gwen's daughter] write more poems?

[1547]   Yours V.W.

Т HE AFFAIR BETWEEN Virginia and Vita Sackville-West began in December 1925. They met another six times before Vita left with her husband Harold Nicolson for Persia, a journey that lasted in all four months. Prolonged separation, however, merely deepened Vita's hold on Virginia's imagination. Her welcome return began again the exchange of affectionate badinage.

LEFT: Lady in a Red Hat, *a portrait of* Vita Sackville-West *by the well-known society painter, William Strang.*

Their relationship lasted even after the moment of passion had passed. Virginia herself seems to have drawn the boundaries around it, which allowed her and Vita to experience intimacy but also keep their respective marriages intact.

TO VITA SACKVILLE-WEST

Tuesday, January 26th, 1926   52 Tavistock Sqre, [W.C.1]

Your letter from Trieste came this morning—But why do you think I don't feel, or that I make phrases? "Lovely phrases" you say which rob things of reality. Just the opposite. Always, always, always I try to say what I feel. Will you then believe that after you went last Tuesday—exactly a week ago—out I went into the slums of Bloomsbury, to find a barrel organ. But it did not make me cheerful. Also I bought the Daily Mail—but the picture is not very helpful. And ever since, nothing important has happened— Somehow its dull and damp. I have been dull; I have missed you. I do miss you. I shall miss you. And if you don't believe it, your a longeared owl and ass. Lovely phrases?

You were sitting on the floor this time last week, where Grizzle is now. Somehow, as you get further away, I become less able to visualize you; and think of you with backgrounds of camels and pyramids which make me a little shy. Then you will be on board ship: Captains and gold lace: portholes, planks—Then Bombay where I must have had many cousins and uncles. Then Gertrude Bell—Baghdad. But we'll leave that, and concentrate upon the present. What have I done? Imagine a poor wretch sent back to school. I have been very industrious, no oranges picked off the top of a Christmas tree; no glittering bulbs. For one thing, you must have disorganised my domesticity, so that directly you went, a torrent of duties discharged themselves on top of me: you cant think how many mattresses and blankets new sheets pillowcases, petticoats and dustpans I haven't had to buy. People say one can run out to Heals and buy a mattress: I tell you it ruins a day; 2 days: 3 days—Every time I get inside a shop all the dust in my soul rises, and how can I write next day? Moreover, somehow my incompetence, and shopkeepers not believing in me, harasses me into a nagging harpy. At last, at last,—but why should I go through it again? I sold 4 mattresses for 16 shillings; and have written I think 20 pages. To tell you the truth, I have been very excited, writing. I have never written so fast [*To the Lighthouse*]. Give me no illness for a year, 2 years, and I would write 3 novels straight off. It may be illusion, but (here I am rung up: Grizzle barks:

settles in again—it is a soft blue evening and the lights are being lit in Southampton Row: I may tell you that when I saw crocuses in the Sqre yesterday, I thought May: Vita.) [Vita was to return from Persia mid-May.] What was I saying: Oh only that I think I can write now, never before—an illusion which attends me always for 50 pages. But its true I write quick—all in a splash; then feel, thank God, thats over. But one thing—I will not let you make me such an egoist. After all, why don't we talk about *your* writing? Why always mine, mine, mine? For this reason, I expect—that after all you're abundant in so many ways and I a mere pea tied to a stick.

(Do you see how closely I am writing? That is because I want to say a great many things, yet not to bore you, and I think, if I write very close, Vita won't see how long this letter is, and she won't be bored) Have I seen anyone? Yes, a great many people, but by way of business mostly—Oh the grind of the Press has been rather roaring in my ears. So many manuscripts to read, poems to set up, and letters to write, and Doris Daglish to tea—A poor little shifty shabby shuffling housemaid, who ate a hunk of cake, and had the incredible defiance and self confidence which is partly lack of Education; partly what she thinks genius, and I a very respectable vivacious vulgar brain. "But Mrs Woolf, what I want to ask you is—have I in your opinion enough talent to devote my life entirely to literature?" Then it comes out she has an invalid father to keep, and not a halfpenny in the world. Leonard, after an hour of this, advised her, in his most decided voice, to become a Cook. That set her off upon genius and fiction and hope and ambition and sending novels to Tom Eliot and so—and so. Off she went, to Wandsworth; and we are to read her essay on Pope. . . .

Now Vita's getting bored in Bombay; but its a bald prosaic place, full of apes and rocks, I think: please tell me; you cant think how, being a clever

FAR LEFT, ABOVE LEFT, CENTRE AND
ABOVE: *Virginia Woolf in the garden at
Garsington, from Lady Ottoline Morrell's
album.*

woman, as we admit, I make every fragment you tell me bloom and
blossom in my mind.

As for the people I've seen, I've fallen in love with none—but thats not
exactly my line. Did you guess that? I'm not cold; not a humbug; not
weakly; not sentimental. What I am; I want you to tell me. Write, dearest
Vita, the letters you make up in the train. I will answer everything. . . .

Now I must finish, for I have to do my lecture for the school at Hayes
Common on Saturday. Mary offers to lend me her motor: but no; I wont. I
want Vita's motor; I want to be nicely treated by her; and I shant be.

Couldn't you write me lots more letters and post them at odd stations as
you pass through?

But of course (to return to your letter) I always knew about your standoffishness. Only I said to myself, I insist upon kindness. With this aim in view, I came to Long Barn. Open the top button of your jersey and you will see, nestling inside, a lively squirrel, with the most inquisitive habits, but a dear creature all the same—

Your Virginia

Are you perfectly well? Tell me.
[1613]

TO VITA SACKVILLE-WEST

[15 July 1926]   52 Tavistock Square, W.C.1

Dear Mrs Nicolson,

This is only business, not affection—I suppose you're not coming to see me; so please, as a darling, send me (oh but better far come and bring me—)
(1) Tennyson by H. N[Harold Nicolson].
(2) *Venetian Glass Nephew* the authoress said severely "Really! Not read any of my books!" Oh what an evening! I expected a ravishing and diaphanous dragonfly, a woman who had spirited away 4 husbands, and wooed from buggery the most obstinate of his adherents: a siren; a green and sweetvoiced nymph—that was what I expected, and came a tiptoe in to the room to find—a solid hunk: a hatchet minded, cadaverous, acid voiced, bareboned, spavined, patriotic nasal, thick legged American. All the evening she declaimed unimpeachable truths; and discussed our sales: hers are 3 times better than mine, naturally; till thank God, she began heaving on her chair and made a move as if to go, gracefully yielded to, but not, I beg you to believe, solicited, on our parts. Figure my woe, on the stairs, when she murmured, "Its the *other* thing I want. Comes of trying to have children. May I go in there?" So she retired to the W.C., emerged refreshed; sent away her cab, and stayed another hour, hacking us to pieces. But I must read her book. . . .

Ever, dear Mrs N.

[1655]   Your devoted Virginia Woolf.

ABOVE: *The American novelist, Elinor Wylie.*

THE HOGARTH PRESS

Venetian Glass Nephew (1925) was the most recent novel by the American novelist and poet, Elinor Wylie (1885–1928). (Elinor Wylie was married three times, not four as Virginia states in her letter. This is not the only detail on which Virginia's imagination took flight.)

TO VITA SACKVILLE-WEST

[19 November 1926]   52 Tavistock Sqre, [W.C.1]

... But you dont see, donkey West, that you'll be tired of me one of these days (I'm so much older) and so I have to take my little precautions. Thats why I put the emphasis on 'recording' rather than feeling. But donkey West knows she has broken down more ramparts than anyone. And isnt there something obscure in you? There's something that doesn't vibrate in you: It may be purposely—you dont let it: but I see it with other people, as well as with me: something reserved, muted—God knows what. Still, still, compare this 19th Nov—with last, and you'll admit there's a difference. It's in your writing too, by the bye. The thing I call central transparency—sometimes fails you there too. I will lecture you on this at Long Barn. Oh why does [Robert] Bridges say my essays are poor, and Mr [Goldsworthy Lowes] Dickinson say I'm the finest critic in English literature? I cannot believe that anybody has ever been so mis-rated as I am: and it makes it much harder to go full tilt at fiction or essays: Let them damn my novels, and I'd do essays: damn essays and I'd do novels. This is one of those glib lies one's pen slips out: of course I shall go on doing precisely what I want. Only with me two inches in the top are so tremendously susceptible. Darling donkey West—will you come at 2.30—to the Press, I think: and then how nice I shall lie on the sofa and be spoilt. But my pain is going already. Was Irene [Cooper Willis, barrister, writer and feminist] nicer than I am? Do you know this interesting fact. I found myself thinking with intense curiosity about death? Yet if I'm persuaded of anything, it is of mortality—Then why this sense that death is going to be a great excitement?—something positive; active?
[1687]   Yr VW.

ABOVE: 'Orlando at the Present Time', a photograph of Vita Sackville-West from Virginia's Orlando, a fictional biography for which Vita was the inspiration.

THE HOGARTH PRESS

TO VITA SACKVILLE-WEST

March 23rd 1927   52 Tavistock Sqre. [W.C.1]

Dearest Honey, (...)

Are you well? Did you enjoy the [Bakhtiari] walk? Were you drowned, shot, raped, tired? Lord, I'd give a great deal to know. But the silly thing is that I'm writing before you've even left Teheran, I suppose. What I pretend to be past is all in the future. . . .

Why do I think of you so incessantly, see you so clearly the moment I'm in the least discomfort? An odd element in our friendship. Like a child, I think if you were here, I should be happy. Talking to Lytton the other night he suddenly asked me to advise him in love—whether to go on, over the precipice, or stop short at the top. Stop, stop! I cried, thinking instantly of you. Now what would happen if I let myself go over? Answer me that. Over what? you'll say. A precipice marked V.

I had a visit from Edith Sitwell whom I like. I like her appearance—in red cotton, many flounced, thought it was blowing a gale. She has hands that shut up in one's own hands like fans—far more beautiful than mine. She is like a clean hare's bone that one finds on a moor with emeralds stuck about it. She is infinitely tapering, and distinguished and old maidish and hysterical and sensitive. She told me awful Brontë stories about being cursed by her mother as a child and made to kill blue bottles in a hot room. I like talking to her about her poetry—she flutters about like a sea bird, crying so dismally. But honey, can one make a new friend? Can one begin new intimate relations? Dont mistake me. No precipice in this case—Only I was discussing friendship with Morgan Forster. One cannot follow up human relations any more he said. Theres Dante to read. Solitude—ones soul. He is half a monk. An elderly bugger is always something of a priest. Leonard went down to Sevenoaks with puppy. Louise [Genoux] met him and Leonard was very downcast Puppy didn't seem to mind going he said. Half laughing I said I'd ring up and ask after her. He took it quite seriously. This shows where you've led us in dog worshipping. He thinks she's hermaphrodite: Lizzy has the flux: puppy still hermetically sealed. . . .

[1735]   Yr Virginia

THE HOGARTH PRESS

TO VITA SACKVILLE-WEST

Friday [13 May 1927]   52 Tavistock Square, [W.C.1]

Darling Vita,

What a generous woman you are! Your letter has just come, and I must answer it, though in a chaos. (Nelly returning: her doctor; her friends; her diet etc) I was honest though in thinking you wouldn't care for [To] The Lighthouse: too psychological; too many personal relationships, I think. (This is said not of the dummy copy) The dinner party the best thing I ever wrote: the one thing that I think justifies my faults as a writer: This damned 'method'. Because I dont think one could have reached those particular emotions in any other way. I was doubtful about Time Passes. It was written in the gloom of the Strike: then I re-wrote it: then I thought it impossible as prose—I thought you could have written it as poetry. I don't know if I'm like Mrs Ramsay: as my mother died when I was 13 probably it is a child's view of her: but I have some sentimental delight in thinking that you like her. She has haunted me: but then so did that old wretch my father: Do you think it sentimental? Do you think it irreverent about him? I should like to know. I was more like him than her, I think; and therefore more critical: but he was an adorable man, and somehow, tremendous. . . .

But why do you think me "lonely". Lovely I understand: not altogether, lonely.

Yes, its an immense relief that you like it; I had been sure you wouldn't. I have so many more books in my head that I should be unhappy to think the whole progeny was doomed to drive us further asunder. The next will be better than this I think. An old creature writes to say that all my fauna and flora of the Hebrides is totally inaccurate. Dear me! whats to be done about it? . . .

So dearest, train, Wednesday, to arrive for dinner. I rushed into a whore's shop in Leicester Sqre and bought a coat.

Come here any time you like . . .

[1754]
                                        VW.
                                (oh I forgot—
                                Virginia Woolf)

LEFT: Edith Sitwell photographed by Cecil Beaton. Edith Sitwell was renowned for her extravagent clothes and sometimes bizarre jewellery. She thought that most English women dressed as if they had been mice in some previous incarnation and once said: 'If one is a greyhound, why try to look like a pekinese?'

THE HOGARTH PRESS

TO VANESSA BELL

Sunday—22nd May 1927   Monk's House, Rodmell,
[Sussex]

ABOVE: *The door of Clive Bell's study at Charleston, decorated by Duncan Grant.*

. . . Then I went to Oxford to speak to the youth of both sexes on poetry and fiction. They are young; they are callow; they know nothing about either—They sit on the floor and ask innocent questions about Joyce— They are years behind the Cambridge young, it seemed to me; Quentin and Julian could knock them into mud pies. But they have their charm . . . They're oddly under our thumb, at the moment—at least this particular group. Roger, the old wizard, has them all entranced—I pretended to a degree of intimacy which, alas, is not mine, to colour my cheeks for them. Clive, they said, was very good fun; but we always feel Roger Fry's the real mind. Then there was Vita, very striking; like a willow tree; so dashing, on her long white legs with a crimson bow; but rather awkward, forced indeed to take her stockings down and rub her legs with ointment at dinner, owing to midges—I like this in the aristocracy. I like the legs; I like the bites; I like the complete arrogance and unreality of their minds—for instance buying silk dressing gowns casually for £5 and then lunching off curd cream (a yellow mess) which she picked out of a tartlet with a fork, dropping the pastry back into the dish; and then tipping porters a shilling for doing nothing; and then—the whole thing (I cant go into details) is very splendid and voluptuous and absurd. Also she has a heart of gold, and a mind which, if slow, works doggedly; and has its moments of lucidity—But enough—You will never succumb to the charms of any of your sex—What an arid garden the world must be for you! What avenues of stone pavements and iron railings! Greatly though I respect the male mind, and adore Duncan (but, thank God, he's hermaphrodite, androgynous, like all great artists) I cannot see that they have a glowworm's worth of charm about them—The scenery of the world takes no lustre from their presence. They add of course immensely to its dignity and safety: but when it comes to a little excitement . . . ! (I see that you will attribute all this to your own charms in which I daresay you're not far wrong). . . .

[1760]   Yr B

ABOVE: *Painted table-top by Duncan Grant and Vanessa Bell, commissioned by the* Woolfs *for Monk's House in the early 1930s.*

LEFT: The fireplace in *Virginia's bedroom at Monk's House*, with tiles specially made by *Vanessa* and inscribed '*VW from VB 1930*'. The lighthouse and ship allude to *Virginia's* novel To the Lighthouse, published in 1927.

THE HOGARTH PRESS

TO ROGER FRY

May 27th 1927   52 Tavistock Sqre, [W.C.1]

My dear Roger,

Thank you very much for your letter. I am immensely glad that you like the Lighthouse. Now I wish I had dedicated it to you. But when I read it over it seemed to me so bad that I couldn't face asking you. And then, as it happened, that very day, I met you somewhere,—was so overcome (did you guess it?) by your magnificence, splendour and purity (of intellect, not body) that I went home and was positive it was out of the question— dedicating such a book to such a man. Really therefore the not-dedication is a greater compliment than the dedication would have been—But you shall have a private copy, if you'll accept it. What I meant was (but would not have said in print) that besides all your surpassing private virtues, you have I think kept me on the right path, so far as writing goes, more than anyone—if the right path it is.

I meant *nothing* by The Lighthouse. One has to have a central line down the middle of the book to hold the design together. I saw that all sorts of feelings would accrue to this, but I refused to think them out, and trusted that people would make it the deposit for their own emotions—which they have done, one thinking it means one thing another another. I can't manage Symbolism except in this vague, generalised way. Whether its right or wrong I don't know, but directly I'm told what a thing means, it becomes hateful to me.

I did not consciously think of Nessa when I was doing Mrs Ramsay. In fact she and my mother seemed to me very different people. But no doubt something of Nessa leaked in. After all, my mother died when I was 13, so that the idea must have been developed somehow. But the whole process of writing remains to me a complete mystery; the only thing I realise is that at last, for some reason, I am beginning to write easily, which may be a sign of decay, of course. I turn to your essays to find out; of course, some one has stolen them, some black-hearted devil. I was just saying to myself now I will read Roger through properly, and you're nowhere to be found. A starved young man—but I forget who—begged it of me one day—

ABOVE: *Photograph of Roger Fry, c. 1925, from Virginia's biography of him published in 1940. Writing in her diary Virginia noted: 'What a curious relation is mine with Roger at this moment—I who have given him a kind of shape after his death. Was he like that? I feel very much in his presence at the moment; as if I were intimately connected with him: as if we together had given birth to this vision of him: a child born of us. Yet he had no power to alter it. And yet for some years it will represent him.'*

thats all I remember. So you must come back, and let us have an argument in person.

London is rather a grind—nice people and nasty people stuck together in bunches, so that one cant get at them separately but has to bolt them whole. I get a little bothered by the idiocy of most human intercourse,—think I shall retire to Rome. But then there too one would be hooked in to the quarrels and loves of the detestable English. Clive is specially rampant at the moment, rolling in the pigsty after his three months abstinence, and rather a repulsive sight. Its an amazing recantation of all he said 3 months ago, but he's so outspoken and innocent in his queer way one can't object. Love is the only God, he says, and art and fame an illusion, which means, I suppose, that he intends to dine out at the Ivy with Mary every night of his life and never write a word. One sees the top of his bald head disappearing into the waves. I don't think Nessa will be able to fish him out this time.

. . . —and how anyone can be such a fool as to think the mind dull compared with the body, Lord knows. I'm sure I live more gallons to the minute walking once round the square than all the stockbrokers in London caught in the act of copulation. As for you—but I've flattered you enough—and it isn't flattery: its sober truth, which makes it worse. Love to Helen.

[1764]   Yr V.W.

MONK'S HOUSE

ONK'S HOUSE IS situated towards the bottom end of the street that
constitutes Rodmell. The village is some three miles south of Lewes
and almost equidistant from Charleston, the house near Firle that
Vanessa Bell and Duncan Grant had lived in during the latter part of the
1914—18 war and which they continued to use as their house in the country.
Ever since 1919, when they had acquired Monk's House, the Woolfs had
likewise punctuated their year with visits to Sussex, at Christmas, Easter and
during the summer months. Virginia obtained intense pleasure from country
life, from observing Leonard's activities in the garden and from the walks she
took. She abhorred the loss of countryside as suburbia spread and in 1928 the
Woolfs bought a field adjoining their garden in order to protect their view. In
1929 they extended the house, adding two new rooms, one of which
became Virginia's bedroom.

During 1930 she was labouring on her most ambitious book, *The Waves*.
She was also seeing a good deal of Vita Sackville-West and of Dame Ethel
Smyth, the elderly composer whom she first met in February of this year.
Ethel had read *A Room of One's Own* and, with great delight, had found in it sup-
port for her own belief that the creative and professional life of women is
cramped and blighted by accepted conventions. She alighted suddenly in Virginia's life, and with her vigorous manner, lack of inhibitions, vehemence
and refusal to compromise, she knocked through Virginia's reserve and established her right to have immediate access to the younger woman's innermost thoughts. Whilst responding to Ethel's demands, Virginia was at first a
little embarrassed by this new development. 'An old woman of seventy-one
has fallen in love with me,' she wrote to Quentin Bell. 'It is at once hideous
and horrid and melancholy-sad. It is like being caught by a giant crab.'

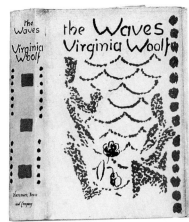

ABOVE: *Dust jacket to Virginia's novel*
The Waves, *published in 1931.*

Nevertheless, she acknowledged Ethel's 'sheer force of honesty' and was drawn by her to discuss in letters topics that she scarcely, if ever, dwelt on with others. Her letters make it apparent that she, in turn, became very dependent on Ethel's mature, good sense; when suicide entered her mind, at first as no more than a theoretical possibility, it was to Ethel she turned for arguments against it.

There was no loss of impetus in Virginia's writing during the 1930s. In the same way that she had thrown off *Orlando* after the more taxing formal and imaginative requirements of *To the Lighthouse*, so she followed *The Waves* with *Flush*, a light tale concerning Elizabeth Barrett Browning's dog. Her next book, *The Years*, revealed a desire to return to the materiality of life which *The Waves* had deliberately ignored. It proved, however, no easy task to readopt more orthodox fictional methods and *The Years* (1937), which took her three years to write, caused much difficulty and a certain amount of despair. Her next publication, *Three Guineas* (1938), pursued ideas first mooted in *A Room of One's Own* but with less persuasive power; her arguments concerning women's rights became mixed with her hatred of Fascism and the governmental and institutional factors that make war possible.

Though for the most part her doubts were confided to her diaries, her letters record moments when panic, fury and depression fissured the smooth tenor of her private life. The woman who one day announced to Leonard that she was the happiest woman alive, could also experience such agony at a social occasion that she was rocked into thoughts of suicide.

TO SAXON SYDNEY-TURNER

27th Feb. [1930]   *52 Tavistock Sqre., [W.C.1]*

My dear Saxon,
    ... What is your opinion of Ethel Smyth?—her music, I mean? She has descended upon me like a wolf on the fold in purple and gold, terrifically strident and enthusiastic—I like her—she is as shabby as a washerwoman and shouts and sings—but the question of her music crops up—I don't mean that she cares what I think, being apparently indomitable in her own

view, but one day you must tell me the truth about it. Anyhow, as a writer she is astonishingly efficient—takes every fence. . . .

[2149] Love Virginia

TO ETHEL SMYTH

22nd April [1930] Monks House, Rodmell,
[Sussex]

Oddly enough—I did precisely the same thing—that is wrote you a long letter and tore it up, owing I think to its egotism. Lord, how furious it makes me to think of the reams you destroyed! Please fish the ashes up . . .

I have just re-lit the fire, in order to be able to write this. And I may tell you that I cooked lunch today and made a loaf of really expert bread. We have our young widow [Mrs Thompsett] half the day—and she goes and leaves us; This is very nearly the ideal life I think; but we have our crosses; I mean people drop in. They are divine people, with whom everything is possible (and how can you suppose that you and your nakedness could shock?—if you heard us—no I'm ashamed even to sketch our bi-sexual conversations. You must revise your estimate of our society radically) Everything is possible I was saying; but I want silence. Today for the first time, I have seen nobody, and my book, a very flickering flame at the moment, begins to draw. I dont know if music needs a shelter round it. Writing is so damnably susceptible to atmosphere. If I could sit here for three months alone, saying the same things, doing the same things, day by day—then perhaps a few pages would be solidly written in the end. As it is, I shall go back to London, and shiver it all to bits. What one wants for writing is habit; I am like one of Leonards fish (we have a pond) which is off at the shadow of a leaf—but I'm egotistical again, and no doubt shall have to burn this. No I cant be bothered to burn it. . . .

[2168] VW.

Virginia was writing The Waves. *She finished the first draft on 29 April and began to rewrite it on 13 June.*

ABOVE: The composer, Dame Ethel Smyth. In 1933 Virginia wrote to her nephew, Quentin: 'Old Ethel meanders so. And she's so deaf. And she's so violent. But she is, to give her her due, very shrewd'.

TO ETHEL SMYTH

Sunday, 22nd June [1930]   [52 Tavistock Square, W.C.1]

O Lord, I have been such a wretch—never to write even a card to thank you for the white flowers. You must have stripped your garden; and then found two huge boxes; and then borne them through Woking on a bicycle; and then up here in a taxi—and I receive all this with only a nod—dear, dear. And it is only on Friday that they were withered. But I buried my nose (why do you like that long proboscis?) 10 times daily in their deliciousness. And thus I was upborne through heaven knows what boredoms. Yes, so I am now saying thank you. . . .

. . . I did not mean, though I must have said, that Leonard had served 7 years for his wife. He saw me it is true; and thought me an odd fish; and went off next day to Ceylon, with a vague romance about us both [Virginia and Vanessa]! And I heard stories of him; how his hand trembled and he had bit his thumb through in a rage; and Lytton said he was like Swift and would murder his wife; and someone else said Woolf had married a black woman. That was my romance—Woolf in a jungle. And then I set up house alone with a brother [Adrian], and Nessa married, and I was rather adventurous, for those days; that is we were sexually very free— . . . but I was always sexually cowardly, and never walked over Mountains with Counts as you did, nor plucked all the flowers of life in a bunch as you did. My terror of real life has always kept me in a nunnery. And much of this talking and adventuring in London alone, and sitting up to all hours with young men, and saying whatever came first, was rather petty, as you were not petty: at least narrow; circumscribed; and leading to endless ramifications of intrigue. We had violent rows—oh yes, I used to rush through London in such rages, and stormed Hampstead heights at night in white or purple fury. And then I married, and then my brains went up in a shower of fireworks. As an experience, madness is terrific I can assure you, and not to be sniffed at; and in its lava I still find most of the things I write about. It shoots out of one everything shaped, final, not in mere driblets, as sanity does. And the six months—not three—that I lay in bed taught me a good deal about what is called oneself. Indeed I was most crippled when I

RIGHT: On the Roof at Brunswick Square by Duncan Grant, painted on the roof of the house that Virginia lived in prior to and immediately after her marriage.

came back to the world, unable to move a foot in terror, after that discipline. Think—not one moment's freedom from doctor discipline—perfectly strange—conventional men; 'you shant read this' and 'you shant write a word' and 'you shall lie still and drink milk'—for six months.

But enough. I must do whatever it is. This is really a letter to thank you for the vast cardboard boxes. How they must have banged about in your third class railway carriage.

[2194]   Virginia

TO ETHEL SMYTH

Wednesday [16 July 1930]   *52 T.[avistock] S.[quare, W.C.1]*

Oh Lord—do all my letters to you begin O Lord?—O Lord again, that was a nice day Ethel. How I enjoyed it and the diversity of my sensations, as we went from solitude to society; and then back; and the wine, and the duck, and the fire—oh and everything; always excepting some twinges of compunction (they came on worse after I had left you) at my own egotistic loquacity. I can assure you I dont romanticise quite freely about myself as a rule—It was only that you pressed some nerve, and then up started in profusion the usual chaos of pictures of myself—some true, others imaginary; more were true than false, I think, but I ought not to have been so profuse. Next time it shall be the other story—yours. But in your benignity and perspicacity—its odd how the image of the soaring aeroplane seeing to the bottom persists—you can penetrate my stumbling and fitful ways: my childish chatter. Yes—for that reason, that you see through, yet kindly, for you are, I believe, one of the kindest of women, one of the best balanced, with that maternal quality which of all others I need and adore—what was I saying?—for that reason I chatter faster and freer to you than to other people. But I wont next time. And you won't think the worse of me, will you? You see, I am, I dont deny it, very excitable. And going home, as the wine went out and a cold sheen appeared on the roofs of Surbiton, I thought, My God what an egoist I am; and that

ABOVE: Ethel Smyth, who told Virginia that in getting to know her, she had felt an emotion comparable only to that which she had experienced on first hearing the music of Brahms. She described Virginia in her diary as being '. . . arrogant, intellectually, beyond words, yet absolutely humble about her own great gift. Her integrity fascinates me.'

was the only twangling wire in the whole composition. I was home by eleven; and slept; and still feel very, extraordinarily well. And I wont therefore accuse Leonard of always castrating my joys. . . .
[2204]   Yr V.

TO ETHEL SMYTH

30th Oct 1930   52 Tavistock Square. [W.C.1]

ABOVE: *A late portrait of Virginia Woolf, by Man Ray.*

Well, I'm glad you caught your train. The guard said to me "She'll drop dead if she tries"—and I'm pleased that you did run, did not drop dead, and did catch the train. It seems to me marvellously gallant and efficient and sensible, as befits the daughter of an officer, and a good omen for the Prison. Its odd how little scenes like that suddenly illumine wherever one may be—Waterloo station. I could swear a ring of light surrounded you me and the guard for one tenth of a second.

Well it was rather a glum, deliberate, middleaged assembly last night [Mrs Woolf's birthday party]—all, oh my word, so much like cuts off one long yard of cake—slice after slice; no beauty, no eccentricity. We stood about in the private room, with bunches of chrysanthemums tied up in orange sashes, and lots of carnations, incredibly unreal, in silver vases. And there were telegrams, cables from Sweden—this was a great prize—and then parcels kept on coming in. And there we all stood about in very inferior evening dress, as was specially requested (not the inferiority—the dress) touching our hair with our hands. At 10 I was discussing with Mrs Harold, who is the black sheep, a divorcée and grown very stout, and the best bridge player in Maidenhead, floods at Staines; at 10.15 I was comparing Harrods and the Army and Navy stores with Mrs Edgar—who has always lived in Putney, and had a bad miscarriage several years ago, since when she has run the Stock Exchange Sweep stakes, and has an alsatian hound which she has painted in oils, "but he has not really that fierce look in his eyes" she says; and then at 10.30 the green baize tables were opened and we played a game called Pink Nines and I, being third won a prize of a plum pudding; and Leonard being Booby won a spotted tie; and at 11 we

ABOVE: *Leonard Woolf, photographed in 1929 in Cassis, from Vanessa Bell's album. Duncan Grant and Vanessa Bell rented a small farm building there during the late 1920s.*

all went into supper (does this bore you) and I sat at the table of honour
with my mother in law—there were four tables, some less honourable
than the others—and cups of soup were handed, anchovy sandwiches
and cold sausage rolls. And then Herbert, the eldest son, rose and drank to
"Our mother, the most marvellous mother, mother in law and friend"
and my mother in law thanked us, "The most perfect, loving and (she
could not remember a third epithet) h.m.m of children" and what I
liked was that though she was all tremors and quivers she ended, like a
child, "And now lets finish our sausage rolls"—this spontaneous bubbling
childishness —witness her passion for chocolate creams and sugar
cakes—being her charm for me. Indeed, in spite of the glumness, grimness,
and oh the intolerable middle class timidity respectability and lack of
accent distinction adventure dash, daring colour—I cant describe to you
the low level of all these childless people, with their uniformity of cars, dogs,
country houses and gardens,—in spite of my damned snobbishness about
them, I always feel slightly warmed and overcome by the entire absense
of pretence, and the goodness, and the rightness—if it is right so to people
the world—of the vast family to which as Herbert said, I have the honour
to belong.

By the way, what are the arguments against suicide? You know what a
flibberti-gibbet I am: well there suddenly comes in a thunder clap a sense of
the complete uselessness of my life. Its like suddenly running one's head
against a wall at the end of a blind alley. Now what are the arguments against
that sense—'Oh it would be better to end it"? I need not say that I have no
sort of intention of taking any steps: I simply want to know—as you are so
masterly and triumphant—catching your train and not running too
fast—what are the arguments against it?

[2265]   V.

*Mrs Woolf, Leonard's mother, was celebrating her eighty-second birthday. Mrs
Harold and Mrs Edgar were her daughters-in-law. The Prison was an oratorio for
soprano, bass-baritone, chorus and orchestra that Ethel Smyth was composing, based
on a philosophic dialogue by H.B. Brewster with whom she had had an affair. It was
first performed in 1931.*

MONK'S HOUSE

TO ETHEL SMYTH

11 March 1931   52 Tavistock Sqre. [W.C.1]

I feel, no doubt wrongly, simply from your voice and what you say mysteriously about 'discipline' that I have annoyed?—no, not annoyed, but perhaps hurt you? Well, I'm so blind and deaf psychologically, that I have to put these, to most people certainties, as questions, and now, because I'm blind and deaf. I'm going to lay before you the reason of the misunderstanding, if there is one. I expect you to ridicule me, but I dont mind being ridiculed, if you understand me, as there is always the chance that you will understand.

It was the party [for Ethel Smyth at Lady Rosebery's]. I dont know when I have suffered more; and yet why did I suffer? and what did I suffer? Humiliation: that I had been dragged to that awful Exhibition of insincerity and inanity against my will (I used to be dragged by my half-brothers against my will—hence perhaps some latent sense of outrage) Then, that you liked the party—you who are uncompromising, truthful, vehement. "Ethel likes this sort of thing" I said, disillusion filled me: all belief fell off me. "And she has planned this, and worse still, subjected me to it. Gulfs separate us." And I felt betrayed—I who have spoken to you so freely of all my weaknesses—I to whom this chatter and clatter on top of any art, music, pictures, which I dont understand,—is an abomination. Oh then, the elderly butlers, peers, champagne, and sugared cakes! It seemed to me that you wantonly inflicted this indignity upon me for no reason, and that I was pinioned there and betrayed and made to smile at your damnation. I who was reeling and shocked, as I see now, (to excuse myself,) by my own struggle with The Waves—who had vainly perhaps but honestly tried to understand you, H.B. [H.B. Brewster, the poet and philosopher with whom Ethel had had an affair and the subject of a memoir by her] the Prison: there I was mocking and mowing, and you forced me to it and you didn't mind it. I went home therefore more jangled and dazed and out of touch with reality than I have been for years. I could not sleep. I took chloral. I spent the next day in a state of horror and disillusion. When you rang me up you seemed to guess at none of all this, and I felt that I could never approach you so as to touch you again. (And without exaggeration you dont know how I have honoured and respected you—come, oddly, to depend upon your sanity) So then I put off [Sybyl] Colefax and Ottoline and resolved to be quit of the posturing and insincerity and being hauled about and made to exhibit myself for ever.

This no doubt seems to you wantonly exaggerated to excuse a fit of temper. But it is not. I see of course that it is morbid, that it is through this even to me inexplicable susceptibility to some impressions suddenly that I approach madness and that end of a drainpipe with a gibbering old man. But this is me; and you can't know me and merely brush this aside and disregard it as a fit of temper. I dont attempt to rationalise; but I can now, after 2 weeks, see how selfish, cold, and indeed brutal I may have seemed to you, when in fact I felt more strongly about you and therefore about your betrayal of me to wolves and vultures than ever before. Excuse this; and continue whatever your scheme may be. I dont suppose I shall understand your explanation, if you give one, or you mine. But I venture it, trusting in your sanity as I do: and because of what I call my respect for you. [2335]   V.

TO ETHEL SMYTH

Sunday [29 March 1931]   52 Tavistock Sqre. [W.C.1]

Just back from the [Sidney] Webbs; and left rather in a fluster, though I enjoyed it—hence can't write a letter. I dont remember saying I wanted a violent letter—though its true I was feeling violent—any letter: you know my tastes. Why did I feel violent, after the [Rosebery] party? It would be amusing to see how far you can make out, with your insight, the various states of mind which led me, on coming home, to say to L:—''If you weren't here, I should kill myself—so much do I suffer.'' (I flatter myself you guessed nothing) . . .
[2341]   Yr V.

The above letter refers again to the agony Virginia had experienced at Lady Rosebery's party. Her reaction to it gives an indication of the difficulties she experienced in moving

ABOVE: *Lady Ottoline Morrell by Cecil Beaton. Virginia Woolf wrote in 1925: 'Ottoline turned up two nights ago, and I was rather overcome by her ravaged beauty, and desperation, and humility.'*

from the solitude necessary for intense creativity into the bright chatter and cultivated artificiality of high society. As this and the next letter show, her states of mind could pass from one extreme to another.

TO ETHEL SMYTH

7th April [1931]   Monks House, [Rodmell, Sussex]

Your letter just come, with a great bundle, from London. We go back—didn't I explain our plans?—on Thursday. But Ethel dear, are you really ill? Why does the dr: prescribe bed for your ears? I am (in spite of the ossified and rigid heart to which you allude) anxious to know the truth . . . more annoyed than you, the woman who takes me for a snake, would think likely. Why, didn't I lie awake last night calming myself out of some momentary fear by inventing your reasons for not being afraid?—And I wrote you a long letter by the way, which was all on the theme of the absurd and irrational happiness of our lives—yes, even poor Leonard, whose breast I pierce daily with hot steel, is divinely happy here; we giggle and joke, and go and poke at roots and plan beds of nasturtium; and altogether, life is a childish happy affair—no reason for happiness, dear me no: and therefore one never talks of it, I suppose: but only of the other state which can be made to sound reasonable. "I'm the happiest woman in England" I said to Leonard yesterday, for no reason, except that we had hot rolls for breakfast and the cat had eaten the chicken. But also the most egotistical—no I think, with all due respect, Ethel's that. Lord, Ethel, did you think I was ever so blind as to say that you, of all people, had conquered egotism? It is only that you ride it so magnificently that one doesn't care if its egotism or altruism—its your uncautiousness I envy; not your selflessness.

Forgive this drivvle. I've been a long walk, have had Nessa Clive and Angelica to tea, and the loudspeaker is pouring forth Wagner from Paris. His rhythm destroys my rhythm; yes, thats a true observation. All writing is nothing but putting words on the backs of rhythm. If they fall off the

ABOVE: Beatrice and Sydney Webb. Their dedication to the Socialist cause impressed Virginia but she found Beatrice Webb a person 'without atmosphere', admirable but also depressing. She once astonished Virginia by declaring marriage a useful 'wastepipe' for the emotions.

LEFT: *Virginia with her niece Angelica, photographed by Lettice Ramsey. Virginia Woolf's fondness for and admiration of her niece caused her to announce:* 'Angelica has spoilt me for other children.'

rhythm one's done—But write I must this evening, because all tomorrow I must be toiling to finish an article on [Edmund] Gosse, whom I hope to hit off smartly, without malice, but without much love either—for he was a crafty, worldly, prim, astute little beast—tomorrow. I've written and written—so many articles—8 to be exact. Five on London; one on Mrs Browning; one on Lockhart; one on Gosse; and all have to be sand papered, made to fit, smoothed, pressed, curled, and sent off before we go. We go on the 16th—and dear me, how glad I shall be to wake up in France and not write. Think of being free from 10 to one to sit and look out of the window!

But when shall I see you? You'll be surprised to hear that I'm in a mood when I should like to hear the particular accent you put on Vir-gin-ia! Shall I come down to Woking one day? Shall we go on with our disquisition? I like this feeling that we are in the middle of a tremendous argument—no, discussion: its not 'seeing' Ethel; its going on with what we were saying last week— ...

[2343]   V.

TO VITA SACKVILLE-WEST

Saturday [8 August 1931]   *Monk's House, [Rodmell, Sussex]*

... Come on *Wednesday* not Tuesday, as early as you can, and stay the night—the chaste night—We have a mint of things to say to you— ... As for Katherine [Mansfield], I think you've got it very nearly right. We did not ever coalesce; but I was fascinated, and she respectful, only I thought her cheap, and she thought me priggish; and yet we were both compelled to meet simply in order to talk about writing. This we did by the hour. Only then she came out with a swarm of little stories, and I was jealous, no doubt; because they were so praised; but gave up reading them not on that account, but because of their cheap sharp sentimentality, which was all the worse, I thought, because she had, as you say, the zest and the resonance—I mean she could permeate one with her quality; and if one felt this cheap scent in it, it reeked in ones nostrils. But I must read her some day. Also, she was for ever pursued by her dying; and had to press on through stages that should have taken years in ten minutes—so that our relationship became unreal also. And there was Murry squirming and oozing a sort of thick motor oil in the background—dinners with them were about the most unpleasant exhibitions, humanly speaking, I've ever been to. But the fact remains—I mean, that she had a quality I adored, and needed; I think her sharpness and reality—her having knocked about with prostitutes and so on, whereas I had always been respectable—was the thing I wanted then. I dream of her often—now thats an odd reflection—how one's relation with a person seems to be continued after death in dreams, and with some odd reality too.

But why be ashamed of wanting a garden and poets? Whats there to be proud of in Fleet Street, and daily papers.

I assure you—only the post is going and I have no time to think what it is that I assure you of—that one walk here fills my poor old head with a sense of such natural happiness as I never get a whole summer in London. And you, being a poet—O how I wish I were!—you being a poet have no use for the odds and ends, the husks, the fragments, the general confusion and vibration which I can make myself believe I find in London. If I were you, I would lie on a bank all day and make one phrase—for Virginia. . . .
[2418]   V.

On 21 January 1932 Lytton Strachey died of cancer. Leonard and Virginia had visited him a week before but he was too ill to see them. For Virginia, Lytton, with his richly stocked mind, penetrating subtlety and anarchic wit, was irreplaceable. In the immediate aftermath she was, like others, concerned as to whether Carrington would be able to come to terms with his death—she had already tried to kill herself shortly before Lytton died and there were very real fears that she would make a second attempt. Carrington was grateful to Virginia for a letter in which she confirmed Carrington's importance in Lytton's life: 'Before he knew you, he was so depressed and restless—and all that changed when you had Tidmarsh.' She also suggested that Carrington

should execute woodcuts for Julia Strachey's novel, *Cheerful Weather for the Wedding*, which the Hogarth Press brought out later that year. Because, like others, they were anxious on her behalf, the Woolfs used this book as an excuse to visit Carrington at Ham Spray in March, after which Virginia wrote the following. Her attempt to forestall despair failed: Carrington shot herself soon after receiving the letter and died six hours later.

ABOVE: *Dora Carrington, Ralph Partridge and Lytton Strachey in the garden at Ham Spray, Lytton's Wiltshire home.*

TO DORA CARRINGTON

Thursday night [10 March 1932] 52 Tavistock Square, W.C.1

Carrington dearest, we are just back [from Ham Spray] and had our dinner, and I cant help scribbling one line to thank you—oh just for being yourself. You cant think how close Lytton comes when you're there: you keep him for me more than anyone. So go on, dearest, devilish though it is for you; because you do what no one else can do. I'm so lonely sometimes without him, so old and futile and merely dried up, and then with you I feel come over me—its so odd—what I was when Lytton was there.

And then its so lovely—the rooms, the carpets, the trees outside, every little object. How do you do it? I felt consoled walking under the trees.

And look what ugly paper this is! When am I going to have the drawings and the book plate?

D'you know there was a coin, silver, Italian or French, in the little box? I must send it back. So good night dearest Carrington, from your attached old friend who would do anything if she could. [2548]

In recognition of Virginia's fondness for Lytton, Carrington had given her a little box which had formerly belonged to Strachey.

ABOVE: *The Ham Spray letterheadings for winter and summer, drawn by Carrington in 1929.*

TO LADY OTTOLINE MORRELL

Tuesday [15 March 1932]   [52 Tavistock Square, W.C.1]

Dearest Ottoline,

I've been away till this evening or I would have written. Yes, of course it was suicide, but at first I didn't like to say so, as they were anxious to get the verdict that it was an accident. She had borrowed a gun from Brian [sic] Guinness, and shot herself early on Friday morning. She died in 3 or 4 hours. Ralph arrived while she was still conscious. She told him it was an accident—that she had been shooting at a rabbit and had slipped. But she had already tried once before when Lytton was dying. That was why we went down—the only chance seemed to be to give her some interruption. But I felt, as we sat talking about Lytton in Lytton's room that afternoon, that she could not go on much longer. She said she had failed with everything except with Lytton—she was very gentle and affectionate. I could only tell her how much we all needed her—indeed, she kept so much of Lytton that her death makes his loss more complete. But she had suffered so terribly and could not believe that there was anything to come in life. I feel that he would have hated it—Pippa [Strachey; sister of Lytton] came back last night on hearing of it. Carrington made every preparation and rang up Ralph after we had gone to say that she felt more cheerful. But it was terrible leaving her alone that night, without anybody in the house. [2553]   yrs Virginia

Bryan Guinness, later to become Lord Moyne, was a friend of Carrington's and she had painted a trompe l'oeil window for his house at Andover. Carrington had visited his home on 29 February, in the company of her husband, Ralph Partridge, Frances Marshall and David Garnett, and had borrowed a gun from him, giving as her reason for doing so the need to shoot rabbits at Ham Spray.

ABOVE: Lytton Strachey by *Vanessa Bell, c. 1912. Virginia and Lytton continued to correspond at intervals but as he lived in the country saw less of each other during the latter part of his life.*

ABOVE: Margery Fry by Claude Rogers, 1939. Margery Fry was the sister of Roger Fry and a prominent figure within educational circles. She was also active within the Howard League for Penal Reform and worked towards the abolition of the death sentence.

ONE OF THE WOOLFS' most successful holidays was their visit to Greece in the spring of 1932. Their companions were Roger Fry and his sister Margery. Margery Fry had grown up under the watchful eyes of her high-minded Quaker parents, Sir Edward and Lady Fry, and, like her five sisters, had never married. But the restrictions imposed on them by their upbringing did not prevent Margery and other of her sisters from becoming forceful, independent and notable figures. Margery did much work with the Howard League for Penal Reform. She also had a considerable reputation in educational circles and became Principal of Somerville College, Oxford. Her brother Roger had a gift for sharing with others his appreciation of art. He was also prone to overwhelming enthusiasms and for that reason was nicknamed 'Old Credulous'. His mental powers had not diminished with age, though he was suffering during the course of this holiday from piles.

ABOVE: Vanessa Bell by Duncan Grant, *painted in the early years of their relationship, before the birth of their daughter Angelica.*

TO VANESSA BELL

Monday, May 2nd [1932]   Delphi,
                                                          [Greece]

. . . Here we are in Delphi, all well except for Roger's inside falling out and my skin peeling in great sores. The wind and sun, the bitter cold and violent heat, the driving all day along rocky or pitted roads, make one feel like a parboiled cactus. All the same, it is so far a great success—I mean from our point of view. No quarrels, no accidents,—in fact, we live in considerable comfort, and have a car to drive in, instead of pottering about in trains and flies as we used. The Inns are now clean as new pins—not a bug, or even a flea to be seen; no corpses on the wall, and the food about as good as English—too many olives and sardines for me; but Leonard and Roger love them and plunge into octopuses and lizards,—I mean they eat them, fried—oily lengths like old rubber tires cut into squares. There's not an English man or woman to be seen; our only society is our own, and some peasants, but as Roger learnt Greek out of the wrong book, most of our talk gets wrong, and when I correct with pure Classical Greek—as my way is—the only result is that we are supposed to have bought 2 kids. No, I haven't probed Margery: old age brings its sad wisdoms—I see one cant eviscerate the elderly unless one wishes to have decomposing carcases hung round one's neck. There is the less need, however, as she has told us all about her emasculated life, with the old Frys—how her father dismissed her lover, and her mother never let her laugh at any story a man told lest it should be thought fast. The dulness of her youth and the 6 sisters was she says worse than a convent. At the age of 97 Lady Fry, having shut them all up in so many band boxes pouring out tea and watering flowers owned that her policy had been a mistake. But it was then too late—Margery has missed having a child, and has to paint and botanise and watch birds and philanthropise for ever instead. I daresay it would be better if she married Roger as you suggest. They hum and buzz like two boiling pots. I've never heard people, after the age of 6, talk so incessantly. Whats more, there's not a word of it what you and I might call foolish: its all about facts, and information and at the most trying moments when Roger's inside is falling down, and Margery must make water instantly or perish, one has only to mention Themistocles and the battle of Platea for them both to become like youth at its spring. The amount they know about art, history, archaeology, biology, stones, sticks, birds, flowers is in fact a constant reproof to me. Margery caught me smiling the other day at my own thoughts and said no Fry had ever done that. ''No'' said Roger, ''we have no power of dissociation.'' which is why of course they're such bad painters—they never simmer for a second. R. has done about 20 pictures under incredible difficulties, but for some reason oil paint wont dry here so they'll all be smudged. As for his amiability and indeed docility its astonishing as he cant walk and cant sit our doings have to be very mild—This is a great mercy—most of the day they paint and we sit about under the trees. I admit we've done most of the museums, but far from thoroughly. The great discovery is that the Greeks were far inferior to the Byzantines. So we search out obscure mosaics and mosques and neglect all we used to see with Violet Dickinson. Lord what ages ago that seems! . . .

Yesterday we had a fine sample of Fry tenacity—Roger had heard of a monastery [Hosios Loukas] with mosaics near Delphi—the driver pointed out that it would add 3 hours to our 10 hour journey, also climbing a mountain at midday on mules. Roger found a shorter way. But, the man said the road is impassable. Not a bit of it said Roger. So it was planned; and we got up at 5 ready to start. At the last moment news came that a car had rolled over the precipice owing to the bad road, and the driver absolutely refused to go. So we compromised and went the long way and rode up the hill in the heat of midday and the mosaics were very inferior and the Monks were very annoying, and we didn't get back to Athens till 8.30 at night, having broken a spring, punctured a tire, and run over a serpent. But we saw an eagle. And Roger said it was only by these experiments that one could get real insight into the people—However he's in the best of tempers: and though we were almost speechless with dust we had a very good dinner and so to bed.

We start back on Monday I think, and shall be home it is thought on the 15th or 16. when the greatest indeed the only pleasure will be to see Dolphin [Vanessa]. I cant think why we dont live in Greece. Its very cheap. The exchange is now in our favour. There has been a financial crisis and we get I dont know how many shillings for our pound. The people are far the most sympathetic I've ever seen. Nobody jeers, or sneers. Everybody smiles. There are no beggars, practically. The peasants all come up across the fields and talk. We can't understand a word and the conflict between Roger's book and Leonards often makes it impossible for us to get a drop to drink, because they cant agree what is the word for wine. . . .

[2578]   B.

TO ETHEL SMYTH

Wednesday May 4th 1932 A.D.   *[Hotel Majestic, Athens]*

. . . I'm sitting on my bed with my ink pot on the po-cupboard, a large boil on my chin, result of wind and sun, a sore-throat, result of cold and dust, but almost perfectly happy all the same. Why did you never tell me that Greece was beautiful? Why did you never mention the sea and the hills and the valleys and the flowers? Am I the only person who has eyes in my head? I solemnly inform you, Ethel, that Greece is the most beautiful country in the whole world; May is the most beautiful season in the whole year; Greece and May together—! There were the nightingales for example

ABOVE: Vanessa Bell, photographed by Lettice Ramsey. The photographer was for a period the girlfriend of Julian Bell. She became a professional photographer, based in Cambridge, and took portraits of some of the most eminent people of this century.

singing in the cypresses where we sat beside the stream: and I filled my lap with scarlet anemones . . .

. . . Roger, whom I meant you to rise at, with his rather cautious admiration of the Greek statues in the museums, is far and away the best admirer of life and art I've ever travelled with; so humane; so sympathetic, so indomitable: though, unfortunately, part of his inside is hanging down, and another part is screwed up, so that he cant ride or walk, and our adventures therefore have to be circumscribed: still as I was saying he never boggles at a terrific expedition like ours yesterday and has nosed out all the Byzantine Churches and Greek Temples (which he thinks sublime: its only the museum statues of muscular boys and cowlike women that remind him of the Royal Academy) and can feel his way along a pillar or a carving or a mosaic with a sensibility and vigour that make one think of a prodigiously fertile spider, where we are ants, hard, shiny, devoid of all filament whatsoever. This faculty of his is a constant marvel to me, and I buttonhole him and say, as at Aegina, "Now Roger tell me why?" and then he quivers his eyes and says how the things a matter of inches—its life, its individuality: thus it differs from Sunium built 6 inches t'other way, as an Arab from a carthorse. Meanwhile Margery his sister has her glass on a bird. An Eagle! I cry. Nonesense. A vulture. She says, or it may be a bee eater. Then Roger shouts, Oh come and look at this! My word thats swell—very swell—and we all gaze up, (This scene takes place at Daphnis in the Byzantine Church) at some annunciation or Crucifixion: and I steal away to the marble door and see the olives and the pines baring their heads and letting the sun and shade darken and illumine them and think how theyre like waves on the grey hill side. . . .

[2579]

VIRGINIA KNEW A great deal about Vita Sackville-West's past life. The following letter shows how intrigued and amused she was to meet Vita's former lover, Violet Trefusis, whose mother, Alice Keppel, had been the mistress of Edward VII. Vita had known Violet since childhood and in 1920, immediately after Violet's marriage to Denys

Trefusis, had eloped with her to France. Their two husbands united to bring about their return.

TO VITA SACKVILLE-WEST

[8? November 1932]   52 T.[avistock] S.[quare, W.C.1]

I'm divinely happy, because I wrote all the morning—Oh how you'll hate my new novel, and how it amuses me!—and then I go for a walk, or drive, and then I come back to tea, carrying one muffin which I eat, with honey, and then I lie on the sofa, and—who d'you think came and talked to me t'other night? Three guesses. All wrong. It was Violet Trefusis—your Violet. Lord what fun! I quite see now why you were so enamoured—then: she's a little too full, now, overblown rather; but what seduction! What a voice—lisping, faltering, what warmth, suppleness, and in her way—its not mine—I'm a good deal more refined—but thats not altogether an advantage—how lovely, like a squirrel among buck hares—a red squirrel among brown nuts. We glanced and winked through the leaves; and called each other punctiliously Mrs Trefusis and Mrs Woolf—and she asked me to give her the Common R. which I did, and said smiling, By the way, are you an Honourable, too?'' No, no, she smiled, taking my point, you, to wit. And she's written to ask me to go and stay with her in France, and says how much she enjoyed meeting me: and Leonard: and we positively must come for a whole week soon. Also Mrs Keppel loves me, and is giving a dinner partly [sic] solely for me in January. How I enjoyed myself! To be loved by Mrs Keppel, who loved, it is said—quite a different pair of shoes.

Well, what I was going to say, but have no time, is that I dont altogether agree with you (on the wireless) about Lawrence. No, I think you exaggerate. Genius, I admit: but not first rate genius. No. And such a cad to Ottoline. My word, what a cheap little bounder he was, taking her money, books, food, lodging and then writing that book. And the other night they broadcast a poem, writer unknown; and L and I listened in; and we said who's that? some modern, quite 2nd rate, but trying to be first rate—pretentious—not genuine. Behold, Lawrence again, so they say. I

ABOVE: Violet Trefusis by Jacques-Emile Blanche, 1926. Her friendship with Vita was the first and most important in a series of intense relationships Vita had with women.

admit the genius, in Sons and Lovers: but thats the sum and pinnacle of it all (I've not read anymore) the rest is all a dilution, a flood, a mix up of inspiration, and prophecy—which I loathe—Oh yes, a genius, but not first rate. So there.

And come and see me

[2660]   V.

Virginia's 'new novel' was The Pargiters, *an attempt to combine fiction with feminist argument in alternating sections. As the book progressed she realized that her initial idea was not viable. She reworked the fiction sections into her novel* The Years, *published in 1937, and expanded the essays into* Three Guineas *(1938).*

In Women in Love, *D.H. Lawrence had cruelly portrayed Ottoline in the character of Hermione.*

ABOVE: *Julian Bell holding his younger brother, Quentin. From Vanessa Bell's album.*

I N 1937 JULIAN BELL, Vanessa's elder son, was killed in the Spanish Civil War. News of his death caused Vanessa to undergo mental and physical breakdown. When she recovered from her initial collapse, she was taken down to Charleston to convalesce. Virginia visited almost daily and her conversation played an important part in Vanessa's recovery. This unexpected development caused a complete reversal in the sisters' relationship, for up till then Virginia had always been the more dependent of the two.

TO VITA SACKVILLE-WEST

[26? July 1937]   52 Tavistock Square, W.C.1.

Dearest Creature,

I was very glad of your letter. I couldn't write, as I've been round with Vanessa all day. It has been an incredible nightmare. We had both been certain he would be killed, and the strain on her is now, perhaps mercifully, making her so exhausted she can only stay in bed. But I think we shall drive her down to Charleston on Thursday.

Lord, why do these things happen? I'm not clear enough in the head to feel anything but varieties of dull anger and despair. He had every sort of gift—above everything vitality and enjoyment. Why must he get set on going to Spain?—But it was useless to argue. And his feelings were so mixed. I mean, interest in war, and conviction, and a longing to be in the thick of things. He was the first of Nessa babies, and I cant describe how close and real and always alive our relation was. As for Nessa—but as I say I'm so stupid what with ordering the char to buy mutton, and generally doing odd jobs I cant think, or as you see write—so forgive this egotism. Shall you come over to M.H. one day? I should like to see you. And dear old Clive,—he is such a pathetic, and always honest, man. cracking his jokes. to try and make us all laugh—wh. I admire
[3285]   Yr V.

I N 1937, VIRGINIA, at Margery Fry's request, began work towards a biography of Roger Fry. Her initial task was to collect as many of his letters as she could find. She talked of her work on these papers with Vanessa, knowing that it would help distract her from her grief at Julian's death.

ABOVE: Julian Bell playing chess with Roger Fry, *Vanessa Bell, c. 1933. Julian was killed in the Spanish Civil War in 1937. Virginia was deeply affected by his death and wrote in her diary that it 'brings close the immense vacancy, and and our short little run into inanity.'*

TO VANESSA BELL

Tuesday [17 August 1937]   Monk's House, [Rodmell, Sussex]

. . . this is only by way of Singe's morning kiss . . . There have been no great adventures to speak of, save that the Bridge [over the River Ouse] was open last night as we came through, in a storm of rain, a sailing ship passing, and all very romantic, and as usual I thought of you. Do you think we have the same pair of eyes, only different spectacles? I rather think I'm more nearly attached to you than sisters should be. Why is it I never stop thinking of you, even when walking in the marsh this afternoon and seeing a great snake like a sea serpent gliding among the grass . . . I'm completely stuck on my war pamphlet [*Three Guineas*] . . . I'm always wanting to argue it with

ABOVE: *Vita Sackville-West, a drawing by William Rothenstein. One of Vita's many achievements was the creation of the famous gardens at Sissinghurst Castle.*

Julian—in fact I wrote it as an argument with him. Somehow he stirred me up to argue—I wish I'd got his essays to read—they might give me some ideas. I suppose Charles [Mauron] will discuss them with you; and I shant see you alone for ever so long. unless I creep over tomorrow, but I hardly think you'll want to see me too soon again. A letter from Tom [Eliot], who wants to come late in September: a letter from a lady who has described me in a French newspaper—"a noble lady with a great shock of white hair"—Lord, are we as old as all that? I feel only about six and a half. And now I must play bowls, be beaten once more, and then have out the scope and see if I can pry into your bedroom. If you notice a dancing light on the water, that's me. The light kisses your nose, then your eyes, and you cant rub it off; my darling honey how I adore you, and Lord knows I cant say what it means to me to come into the room and find you sitting there. Roger felt just the same. Have you noted any extracts in his letters? I think you must begin at the beginning with old Lady Fry [his mother]. So no more.

[3294]   B.

VITA APPEARS TO have been more frightened by the prospect of war than Virginia, who nevertheless was very alert to all the minutiae concerning preparations for war and for people's safety. She watched and observed with a mixture of rage and despondency, aware that if Hitler were to invade Britain she and Leonard would be on the hit list of intellectuals and other undesirables.

TO VITA SACKVILLE-WEST

Tuesday 29th Aug. [1939]   Monk's House, Rodmell, near Lewes,
                                                                                          Sussex.

Well, there's another day of peace—I mean we've just listened in to the P.M. I suppose Harold came back [from the House of Commons], so you didn't come [to Rodmell].

I cant help letting hope break in,—the other prospect is too mad.

But I dont think I'm philosophic—rather, numbed. Its so hot and sunny on our little island—L. gardening, playing bowls, cooking our dinner: and outside such a waste of gloom. Of course I'm not in the least patriotic, which may be a help, and not afraid, I mean for my own body. But thats an old body. And all the same I should like another ten years: and I like my friends: and I like the young. That'll all go forever if—Meanwhile, not a van will come to unpack furniture or remove books at 37 [Mecklenburgh Square]: all's held up: publishing and moving blocked. We go up on Thursday to see whats to be done.

Otherwise come at any time, and indeed, my dearest creature, whatever rung I'm on, the ladder is a great comfort in this kind of intolerable suspension of all reality—something real.

But isn't it odd?—one cant fold it in any words.

[3548]   V.

TO VITA SACKVILLE-WEST

[2nd September 1939]   [Monk's House, Rodmell, Sussex]

Yes, dearest Creature, come at any moment you like and share our pot. Alone today and what a mercy!

I did like your letter. And if I'm dumb and chill, it doesn't mean I dont always keep thinking of you—one of the very few constant presences is your's and so—well no more. Yes, I sit in a dumb rage, being fought for by these children whom one wants to see making love to each other.

So come: and I'll write to you, if to no one else, when ever I've a moment free.

dearest creature, how I go on seeing you, tormented.

[3549]   V.

ABOVE: Virginia Woolf, *water colour and pencil, by Wyndham Lewis.*

V IRGINIA'S BIOGRAPHY OF Roger Fry was published in July 1940. Her novelistic skills worked against her talent as a biographer, for her impressionistic observations jostled uncomfortably with the simultaneous need to marshall a multitude of facts. Not generally regarded as one of her best books, it nevertheless, as she claims in her diary, catches a good deal of Roger Fry's iridescence. The pleasure it afforded others brought her many letters.

ABOVE: Roger Fry reading in the garden at Charleston, 1933. Virginia described Fry as '. . . the most heavenly of men . . . so rich, so infinitely gifted'.

TO R. C. TREVELYAN

12th Aug 1940

Monk's House, Rodmell, near Lewes, Sussex

Dear Bob,

Your letter gave me very great pleasure. You knew Roger long before I did, and in many ways must have known him better. I was terribly afraid that my portrait of him wouldn't seem to you a true one. Its a great relief to me that you and Bessy like it. The difficulties, as you say, were immense. Often I almost gave up in despair. I was so hampered by family feelings (though the Frys have been very kind) and then the mass of letters was bewildering. But I'm glad now, if you think its given something of what Roger was, that I went on with it. I'm specially pleased that Julian was interested—Roger would have liked to attract the younger generation.

We're having—much to our surprise—to print a second edition. I'm sending some of your corrections, but doubt if they'll be in time. If you could let me have the others, I would keep them, in case there should ever be a 3rd edition. Dear me, how careless to let so many creep in: Margery Fry, Leonard and Vanessa, all read the MS: and I hoped it was unusually accurate. . . .

[3626]

Yr ever
Virginia Woolf

Robert Trevelyan, the poet, had been a friend of Roger Fry and had shared a house with him in London soon after Fry came down from Cambridge. Bessy (Elizabeth Trevelyan) was his wife and Julian Trevelyan, a painter, was his son.

TO BENEDICT NICOLSON

13 Aug. 1940   Monk's House, Rodmell,
                                                    Lewes, [Sussex]

Dear Ben,

Just as I began to read your letter, an air raid warning sounded. I'll put down the reflections that occurred to me, as honestly, if I can, as you put down your reflections on reading my life of Roger Fry while giving air raid alarms at Chatham. . . .

Here the raiders came over head. I went and looked at them. Then I returned to your letter. "I am so struck by the fools paradise in which he and his friends lived. He shut himself out from all disagreeable actualities and allowed the spirit of Nazism to grow without taking any steps to check it. . . . " Lord, I thought to myself, Roger shut himself out from disagreeable actualities did he? Roger who faced insanity, death and every sort of disagreeable—what can Ben mean? Are Ben and I facing actualities because we're listening to bombs dropping on other people? And I went on with Ben Nicolson's biography. After returning from a delightful tour in Italy, for which his expensive education at Eton and Oxford had well fitted him, he got a job as keeper of the King's pictures. Well, I thought, Ben was a good deal luckier than Roger. Roger's people were the very devil; when he was Ben's age he was earning his living by extension lecturing and odd jobs of reviewing. He had to wait till he was over sixty before he got a Slade professorship. And I went on to think of that very delightful party that you gave in Guildford Street two months before the war. . . . Then I looked at your letter . . . "This intensely private world which Roger Fry cultivated could only be communicated to a few people as sensitive and intelligent as himself . . . " Why then did Ben Nicolson give these parties? Why did he take a job under Kenneth Clark at Windsor? Why didn't he chuck it all away and go into politics? After all, war was a great deal closer in 1939 than in 1900.

Here the raiders began emitting long trails of smoke. I wondered if I was facing disagreeable actualities; I wondered what I could have done to stop bombs and disagreeable actualities . . . Then I dipped into your letter again.

"This all sounds as though I wish to say that the artist, the intellectual, has no place in modern society. On the contrary, his mission is now more vital than it has ever been. He will still be shocked by stupidity and untruth but instead of ignoring it he will set out to fight it; instead of retreating into his tower to uphold certain ethical standards his job will be to persuade as many other people as possible to think and behave in the same way—and on his success and failure depends the future of the world."

Who on earth, I thought, did that job more incessantly and successfully than Roger Fry? Didn't he spend half his life, not in a tower, but travelling about England addressing masses of people, who'd never looked at a picture and making them see what he saw? And wasn't that the best way of checking Nazism? Then I opened another letter; as it happened from Sebastian Sprott, a lecturer at Nottingham; and I read how he'd once been mooning around the S. Kensington Museum " . . . then I saw Roger. All was changed. In ten minutes he caused me to enjoy what I was looking at. The objects became vivid and intelligible . . . There must be many people like me, people with scales on their eyes and wax in their ears . . . if only someone would come along and remove the scales and dig out the wax. Roger Fry did it . . . "

Then the raiders passed over. And I thought I cant have given Ben the least notion of what Roger was like. I suppose it was my fault. Or is it partly, and naturally, that he must have a scapegoat? I admit I want one. I loathe sitting here waiting for a bomb to fall; when I want to be writing. If it doesn't kill me its killing someone else. Where can I lay the blame? On the Sackvilles. On the Dufferins? On Eton and Oxford? They did precious little it seems to me to check Nazism. People like Roger and Goldie Dickinson did an immense deal it seems to me. Well, we differ in our choice of scapegoats.

But what I'd like to know is, suppose we both survive this war, what ought we to do to prevent another? I shall be too old to do anything but write. But will you throw up your job as an art critic and take to politics? And if you stick to art criticism, how will you make it more public and less private than Roger did? About the particular points you raise; I think if you'll read some of the last articles in *Transformations* [1926] you'll find that

ABOVE: Angelica playing the violin, *by her father, Duncan Grant.*

Roger got beyond the very classical and intellectual painters; and did include Rembrandt, Titian and so on. I've no doubt you're right in saying that his attempts at the sort of Berenson connoiseurship were lamentable. I've never read BB, so I cant say. I did read Roger's last Slade lectures however; and was much impressed by the historical knowledge shown there. But of course I'm not an art critic; and have no right to express an opinion.

Well, the hostile aeroplanes have passed over my head now; I suppose they're dropping bombs over Newhaven and Seaford.

I hope this letter doesn't sound unkind. Its only because I liked your being honest so much that I've tried to be. And of course I know you're having a much worse time of it at the moment than I am . . . Another siren has just sounded.

Yours ever
Virginia Woolf

I'm not sure, on reading this letter over, that I'm right to send it. It sounds too severe. I've been discussing it with Leonard. He says he thinks everybody's to blame for the present condition of the world, but the difficulty is to see what anyone—or in a particular case Roger Fry—could have done, which would have made the slightest difference to what has happened. Equally, I think you'll understand I'm not blaming you; and so send it.

[3627]

Benedict Nicolson was the elder son of Harold Nicolson and Vita Sackville-West. He became Keeper of the King's Pictures and a distinguished editor of the Burlington Magazine, founded by Roger Fry and others in 1903.

A FTER THE DEATH of his wife Ray, David Garnett began living with Angelica, the daughter of Vanessa Bell and Duncan Grant, and eventually married her in 1942. Their union was the cause of distress to her parents, partly because Garnett was twice Angelica's age. Initially Virginia had also been concerned by it, chiefly because of her affection for Vanessa and dread of anything that would cause her more unhappiness. Nothing of all this transpires in the following letter, written to a beloved niece whose upbringing had been made difficult by her mother's protectiveness. A similar tendency to pamper can be found in this letter which is written not to a child but to a young woman of twenty-two years.

TO ANGELICA BELL

Saturday [26 *October* 1940]
*Monk's House, Rodmell,
Lewes, Sussex*

I cant tell you, my darling—this is the way Aunt [Mary] Fisher's letters always began—no, My darling child. . . . I cant tell you what a delight it was to get your and good Brock's [David Garnett] letters. What would Aunt Mary have said to Brock? Well, she'd have forgiven Brock, but she'd never never never have forgiven you. She was a chaste woman—13 children, 4 miscarriages. But why do I waste paper on Aunt Mary?

Yesterday we heard a whistle of bombs as we played bowls, and down they plumped—4 in a row—in the field at the top. All the mothers in Rodmell at once ran screaming: ''The Bus! the Bus!' because the childrens Bus was coming along the road. But God was good; nobody was hurt; and I had the great delight of seeing the smoke and being within an inch of Heaven.

This is a great score over Nessa.

Mummy says she's found you the most perfect house in the most perfect place—oh far better than Rodmell. So of course I'm wild to take it myself —which indeed we must [*sic*] store our furniture somewhere, Meck. Sqre. being a mere splinter of glass, the wind blowing in and out of my cupboards and the books all down. As for 52 Tavistock,—well, where I used to dandle you on my knee, there's Gods sky: and nothing left but one wicker chair and a piece of drugget.

Isn't life a whirligig? But do remember to send me some coloured papers, all the same. Did I tell you about my rug? After an infinity of time,

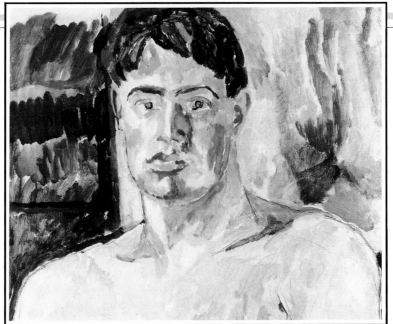

LEFT: David Garnett, by Duncan Grant, 1915. *Grant's sensuous feelings towards Garnett are evident in this portrait, painted at the time when they were having an affair. Garnett lived with Vanessa Bell and Duncan Grant during the First World War, first at Wissett Lodge in Suffolk, and then at Charleston. He was present at Charleston the night Vanessa's third child, Angelica, was born and, in a letter written at the time, remarked that he thought of marrying her. Over twenty years later he did so.*

spent, now writing, now reading, my true gift has at last proved to be rug making. I make rugs of all colours: some say they never wear out. But thats no reason why I shouldn't have your papers. Mummy is altogether flummoxed—danderrydown flummoxed, as she calls it—about your design. Saying this she combed her hair all up the wrong way. It was an awful spectacle. So whats to be done? She says you've got it.

. . . You see when I write to you, I'm almost mistress of the other art of poetry. I daresay you're putting the pot on and wont want to spell out any more. Oh Lord, I've forgotten the fish. What shall we have for dinner? The old mutton once more? But it was never much of a joint in its heyday.

Its a tearing gale, and the Witcherinas are floating past in a roaring rhapsody of circumgyration. So I must wing my way round the Bowling Green. I've just been to see the [bomb] craters. If you look at the moon through a telescope, thats what they're like.

Do thank Brock for his most entirely sustaining and yet so light and yet so nourishing letter: and ask him to write another, only *one* kiss for him though: the rest for me. . . .
[3657]

MONK'S HOUSE

The house Vanessa had found for Angelica and David Garnett was Claverham Farm, Berwick, about four miles from Charleston. They lived there for about nine months.

WITH THE BOMBING of Mecklenburgh Square in September 1940, Virginia no longer had a base in London. It still haunted her imagination, as the following letter reveals.

TO ETHEL SMYTH

12th Jan 41   Monks House, Rodmell,
                                                                      [Sussex]

. . . How odd it is being a countrywoman after all these years of being Cockney! For almost the first time in my life I've not a bed in London. D'you know what I'm doing tomorrow? Going up to London Bridge. Then I shall walk, all along the Thames, in and out where I used to haunt, so through the Temple, up the Strand and out into Oxford Street, where I shall buy maccaroni and lunch. No. You never shared my passion for that great city. Yet its what, in some odd corner of my dreaming mind, represents Chaucer, Shakespeare, Dickens. Its my only patriotism: save one vision, in Warwickshire one spring [May 1934] when we were driving back from Ireland and I saw a stallion being led, under the may and the beeches, along a grass ride; and I thought that is England.

[3678]   V.

AFTER THE BOMBING of Mecklenburgh Square, the Woolfs lived permanently at Rodmell. Virginia welcomed the simpler routine that life in the country encouraged, but in the spring of 1941 there was a marked deterioration in her health. Not wishing to be a burden on Leonard, she drowned herself in the River Ouse on 28 March 1941.

MONK'S HOUSE

TO LEONARD WOOLF

[28 March 1941]   [Monk's House, Rodmell, Sussex]

Dearest,

I want to tell you that you have given me complete happiness. No one could have done more than you have done. Please believe that.

But I know that I shall never get over this: and I am wasting your life. It is this madness. Nothing anyone says can persuade me. You can work, and you will be much better without me. You see I cant write this even, which shows I am right. All I want to say is that until this disease came on we were perfectly happy. It was all due to you. No one could have been so good as you have been, from the very first day till now. Everyone knows that.

V.

You will find Roger's letters to the Maurons in the writing table draw the Lodge. Will you destroy all my papers.
[3710]

Virginia wrote three suicide letters—two to Leonard, one to Vanessa. There is some dispute as to which of the two to Leonard was written first. Both, however, are substantially the same, but the above is more concise, the more definitive.

ABOVE: Leonard Woolf photographed in 1944, three years after Virginia's death.

ABOVE: *Virginia Woolf photographed in 1939 by Gisèle Freund in Tavistock Square. Throughout her life Virginia hated sitting for portraits. In June 1939 Victoria Ocampo brought Freund to see Virginia who reluctantly agreed to sit for her the next day.*

RECIPIENTS

Clive Bell

CLIVE BELL WAS THE son of a Welsh colliery owner and mining engineer. He was educated at Marlborough School and King's College, Cambridge. There he became a friend of Thoby Stephen, who described him to his two sisters as a cross between Shelley and a country squire, for he combined hunting and shooting with a love of poetry and art. On leaving Cambridge he went to Paris for a few months, intending to pursue historical research but in fact spending more time in the company of painters. On his return to England he proposed to Vanessa Stephen and eventually married her. Owing to his friendship with Roger Fry he became caught up in the excitement caused by the arrival of French Post-Impressionism in Britain and he selected the English section for the Second Post-Impressionist Exhibition held in 1912. Though he wrote fairly extensively on art in books and periodicals, his most influential contribution was his book *Art*, published in 1914, which helped to demolish the existing hierarchy of aesthetic values and promoted in its place the concept of 'significant form'. Intrigued by his sister-in-law, he had a brief flirtation with her but, more importantly, encouraged her to write and advised her on her first novel. Her debt to Clive Bell, who convinced her that she was a novelist, seemed to him after her death 'the finest feather I shall ever be able to stick in my cap'.

Vanessa Bell

VIRGINIA WOOLF'S ELDER sister. The bond established between Vanessa and Virginia in childhood remained profound, each sister at regular intervals assessing her progress against that of the other. Such closeness was made possible by Vanessa's decision to deal, not with words, but paint. She trained first under Sir Arthur Cope, then at the Royal Academy Schools. Her desire to be an artist was not weakened by her marriage to Clive Bell in 1907, nor by the arrival of two sons: Julian in 1908 and Quentin in 1910. She reacted strongly to the work of the French Post-Impressionists during the pre-1914 period and joined the avant-garde, using radical simplification in her representational work and briefly experimenting with abstraction. Her later work was less adventurous though it continued to display a subtle responsiveness to relationships of colour and light. Her unique capacity for avoiding acrimony and dispute enabled her to step out of marital relations with Clive Bell, enjoy a brief affair with Roger Fry and finally settle for a life-long companionship with Duncan Grant without losing the loyalty, affection and respect of all three. She also had a child by Duncan Grant – Angelica, who was born in 1918. Vanessa's knack for managing domestic arrangements creatively is one reason why Bloomsbury remained a cohesive group long after the circumstances that had intially brought its members together had vanished.

Gerald Brenan

GERALD BRENAN WAS A friend of Ralph Partridge whom he met whilst serving in the Army during the First World War. Soon after the war ended he took himself off to Spain where he lived on a small inheritance and devoted himself to the study of literature and the art of writing. On return visits to England he met, through Partridge, Dora Carrington with whom he fell in love and had an affair. Leonard and Virginia Woolf visited him in Spain for a fortnight in the spring of 1923 and, according to Virginia, they discussed literature twelve hours a day. The arguments that she had with Brenan about literature were continued afterwards in a succession of letters. In 1931 he married the American Gamel Woolsey. He also published several books, including a history of Spanish literature (1935) and three volumes of autobiography, the first volume of which, *South from Granada*, contains an account of the Woolf's 1923 visit.

Dorothy Brett

THE HON. DOROTHY BRETT was the daughter of Lord Esher. Brett, as she was familiarly known, had trained at the Slade School of Art with Dora Carrington and Mark Gertler. She met Virginia Woolf at Garsington, the home of Lady Ottoline Morrell, but the two were not close friends. Her interest, for Virginia, lay partly in her friendship with Katherine Mansfield, with whom for a time she was closely affiliated. She also became devoted to D. H. Lawrence, to such an extent that when he left England for Mexico she followed and set up home close to him and his wife Frieda. She remained living there after he died, becoming a local celebrity and continuing to paint.

Dora Carrington

DORA CARRINGTON STUDIED painting at the Slade School of Art with Barbara Bagenal (née Hiles) and Mark Gertler who fell in love with her. She rejected Gertler in favour of the homosexual Lytton Strachey and set up house with him, first at Tidmarsh, near Pangbourne, then at Ham Spray in Wiltshire. Their life together was complicated by Lytton's love for Ralph Partridge who in turn fell in love with Carrington. To please Lytton, Carrington married Ralph and all three lived in a *ménage à trois*. She continued to paint and undertake decorative work even though the predominantly literary environment in which she lived gave little encouragement to her talents.

Margaret Llewelyn Davies

MARGARET LLEWELYN DAVIES was closely involved in the Women's Suffrage movement and was Secretary of the Women's Co-operative Guild. Virginia Woolf admired her capacity for public speaking, her vitality and vigour. She was a friend, not only of Virginia, but also of Leonard Woolf and helped stimulate his interest in the Labour movement. This proved of crucial importance during the Woolfs' early married life, for it helped distract Leonard from the anxieties caused by Virginia's mental illness. Some years later Virginia wrote to Margaret Llewelyn Davies: 'You saved Leonard I think, for which I shall always bless you, by giving him things to do. It seems odd, for I know you so little, but I felt you had a grasp on me, and I could not utterly sink.' This and other letters bear out Virginia's affection for her.

Violet Dickinson

A QUAKER WITH ARISTOCRATIC connections, Violet Dickinson had been a close friend of Virginia's half-sister, Stella Duckworth. After Stella's death, she continued to befriend the Stephen children, becoming a person of especial importance for Virginia. Rake-thin and six feet tall, she was warm-hearted, unpretentious and a spirited contributor to any social occasion. She was also one of the first to admire and encourage Virginia's talent for writing and helped place her first published articles and reviews in *The Guardian*, a weekly newspaper catering for a clerical public. She also fulfilled a maternal role, offering sympathy and stability, and looked after Virginia during the latter's second mental breakdown—and subsequent suicide attempt—in 1904. Virginia fell in love with her and filled her letters to Violet with passionate remarks, jokes and endearments. Though her later letters reveal a slight irritation with Violet's inconsequential style of letter writing, she never forgot her debt to this large and large-hearted woman.

Roger Fry

PAINTER, ART CRITIC AND entrepreneur, Roger Fry organized the two famous Post-Impressionist exhibitions, held in 1910 and 1912, which effectively introduced England to modern art. A man of abundant interests and talents, he had a varied career, as Virginia Woolf later recorded in her biography of him published in 1940. His Quaker background had fostered his ability to stand apart from received opinion. Virginia Woolf was inspired and stimulated by his questing intelligence, admitted her debt to him as a writer and at one point thought of dedicating her novel, *To the Lighthouse*, to him. She did not do so, she later explained to him, because at the last moment she doubted the book's worth.

Lady Ottoline Morrell

AN ARISTOCRAT OF IMPRESSIVE mien, Lady Ottoline was compared by Virginia Woolf to the Spanish Armada in full sail. She lived with her husband, Philip Morrell, in London and at Garsington, in Oxfordshire, where she gave hospitality to many artists and writers. Her generosity was not always returned; D. H. Lawrence, for instance, put a cruel portrait of her, as Hermione, into *Women in Love*. Her extravagant personality made her a figure larger than life. Though much laughed at behind her back, by Virginia and others, she had an undeniable grandeur that soared above all conventions.

Jacques Raverat

A FRENCH PAINTER WHO WAS educated in England. He first met Virginia Woolf in 1911 when he became engaged to her friend, Gwen Darwin. They settled in Vence, in the South of France, and Virginia began corresponding regularly with Jacques in the 1920s. In 1924 she learnt that he was dying slowly of multiple sclerosis. He continued to write to her, dictating his letters to his wife, and she in turn shared with him some of her most intimate thoughts about writing, art and literature. Virginia admired his uncompromising reality, his 'hard, truculent mind', ('so clear cut, and logical and intense') and sent him proofs of *Mrs Dalloway* for his opinion. His reply, written just before his death, gave her 'one of the happiest days of my life'.

Vita Sackville-West

THE ONLY CHILD OF Lord Sackville and his half-Spanish wife, Vita Sackville-West grew up at Knole, the baronial country house near Sevenoaks. She married the writer and diplomat, Harold Nicolson, by whom she had two sons, Benedict and Nigel. Their married life was conducted on unorthodox lines, both engaging in affairs with their own sex whilst remaining deeply devoted to each other. Vita achieved eminence as a poet, novelist, travel-writer, broadcaster and journalist. She also created an outstanding garden at her home, Sissinghurst Castle in Kent. For Virginia Woolf she had undeniable glamour. One image that she never forgot was gained whilst they were shopping together in Sevenoaks: 'she shines in the grocer's shop . . . with a candle lit radiance, stalking on legs like beech trees, pink glowing, grape clustered, pearl hung.' Virginia commemorated her love for Vita in *Orlando* which was composed from details in Vita's life and family background.

Ethel Smyth

THE DAUGHTER OF A GENERAL, Ethel Smyth studied music at the Leipzig Conservatory. As a woman composer she experienced great difficulties, which she recorded in her autobiographies, in getting her music performed. Her best-known work is *The Wreckers*, a three-act opera, first performed in Leipzig in 1906 and in Britain in 1909. She involved herself with the Women's Suffrage movement and her *March of the Women* frequently accompanied Women's Social and Political Union processions. After living for some years on the Continent, she settled in England. Her music ('slashing stuff', as an admirer remarked of her Mass) remained Germanic in inspiration. She based one of her operas on a W. W. Jacobs story, and based the libretto for *The Prison*, an oratorio for soprano, bass-baritone, chorus and orchestra, on a poem by H. B. Brewster with whom she had an affair. *The Prison* was first performed in 1931, the year after she met Virginia Woolf. By then in her seventies, she became Virginia Woolf's most dedicated admirer and drew from her some of her most interesting letters. Ethel Smyth was herself a spirited prose-writer, producing a number of books besides her autobiographies. As Hilda Tablet, she is the subject of affectionate parody in a radio series by Henry Reed.

Lytton Strachey

BIOGRAPHER, ESSAYIST AND critic. Like the Stephens, Lytton Strachey came from a highly intellectual family and was a cousin of Duncan Grant. He met Thoby Stephen at Cambridge and took part in the Thursday evening 'at homes' at 46 Gordon Square where, with his acerbity, wit and love of bawdiness, he was a significant influence upon the creation of Bloomsbury. He never disguised his homosexuality but in 1909 he proposed to Virginia Stephen and was accepted. Both quickly realized the impossibility of this union and, as Quentin Bell has said, 'They contrived a gentle disengagement.' Lytton's first book, *Landmarks in French Literature* (1912), displayed his wide reading, but far more significant was his next publication, *Eminent Victorians* (1918), which acted as a reproof to the feeble critical standards that prevailed in the practice of biography, and replaced hagiography with an insidious, questioning irony. Virginia Woolf's respect for Lytton did not prevent her from occasionally finding fault with his writing. Nevertheless her recognition of his importance drew her closer to Dora Carrington with whom he lived.

Saxon Sydney-Turner

ONE OF THOBY STEPHEN's Cambridge friends, Saxon Sydney-Turner became a regular visitor to 46 Gordon Square and an intimate member of Bloomsbury. His reputation for erudition was enhanced by his silence. He could pick up a Greek author and translate a passage aloud as he read. He also had a formidable knowledge of music. But his talent never found a suitable outlet and he buried his gifts in the Civil Service, his brilliance proving ultimately sterile. He fascinated Virginia who puzzled over his eccentricities and was moved by his pathos which became more pronounced when Barbara Hiles, the love of his life, rejected him in favour of Nicholas Bagenal.

Madge Vaughan

THE DAUGHTER OF the writer John Addington Symonds, Madge Vaughan had married one of Virginia Woolf's cousins, William Wyamar Vaughan, a schoolmaster. She was for Virginia a romantic figure trapped in unsympathetic circumstances, for as a schoolmaster's wife she was obliged to lead a life very different from that which she had enjoyed as her father's child, brought up in a liberal environment in the Swiss mountains. She was passionately interested in the arts and had aspirations as a writer. Virginia sent her some of her early thoughts on writing and also fell in love with her, later using her as the model for Sally in *Mrs Dalloway*.

BIBLIOGRAPHY

The works of Virginia Woolf were all first published by the Hogarth Press unless otherwise stated.

Novels

The Voyage Out (Duckworth, 1915)
Night and Day (Duckworth, 1919)
Jacob's Room (1922)
Mrs Dalloway (1925)
To the Lighthouse (1927)
Orlando: A Biography (1928)
A Room of One's Own (1929)
The Waves (1931)
Flush: A Biography (1933)
The Years (1937)
Three Guineas (1938)
Between the Acts (1941)

Short Stories

The Mark on the Wall (1917)
Kew Gardens (1919)
Monday or Tuesday (1921)
A Haunted House and other Short Stories (1943)

Essays

The Common Reader (1925)
The Common Reader: Second Series (1932)
The Death of the Moth and Other Essays (1942)
The Moment and Other Essays (1947)
The Captain's Death Bed and Other Essays (1950)
Granite and Rainbow (1958)
Contemporary Writers (1965)

Biography

Roger Fry: A Biography (1940)

Miscellaneous

A Writer's Diary (Extracts from the Diary of Virginia Woolf, edited by Leonard Woolf, 1953)

INDEX

Numbers in italics refer to illustration captions. 'VW' refers to Virginia Woolf.

ACKNOWLEDGEMENTS

We are grateful to Virginia Woolf's executors, Professor Quentin Bell and Mrs Angelica Garnett, and to Chatto and Windus for permission to extract material from *The Letters of Virginia Woolf*, edited by Nigel Nicolson and his assistant Joanne Trautmann, and originally published by the Hogarth Press between 1975 and 1980. The editor of this present edition wishes to express particular gratitude to Nigel Nicolson and Joanne Trautmann for the insights and scholarship established by their work. At the end of every letter in this book a number in square brackets will be found which relates to the numbering used in Nicolson and Trautmann's six-volume edition. We have checked that the letters here printed do not repeat any printer's errors found in the original publication, and the reader can therefore assume that irregularities in spelling or punctuation are those used by Virginia Woolf.

This book is primarily intended as an introduction to Virginia Woolf, the letter writer. The reader wanting to know more about Virginia Woolf's life will find it admirably dealt with by Quentin Bell in his two-volume biography. Virginia Woolf's diary, impeccably edited by Anne Olivier Bell, acts as the counterpart to her letters and will deepen the reader's understanding both of her life and her creativity.

The illustrations are reproduced by kind permission of the following:
© ADAGP, Paris and DACS, London, 1991 (for the work of Man Ray), 6, 121 (left); The Bloomsbury Workshop, London 10, 60, 61, 63, 66, 67, 69, 92/3; Bridgeman Art Library 131, 139 (Victoria & Albert Museum); Joanna Carrington 28; The Charleston Trust 14, 26, 27, 31, 35, 38, 58, 110, 140; Anthony d'Offay Gallery, London 11, 12, 30, 47, 49, 55, 59, 91, 92, 93, 94, 96, 99, 119, 130, 145; Glasgow Museums and Art Galleries 102; Philip H.R. Goodman and Adrian M. Goodman 56, 61, 65, 104, 105; Sophie Gurney 71, 85, 88, 89, 97; John Hillelson Agency 146; Hulton Picture Company 1, 23, 73, 79, 101, 106, 120, 147; Provost and Scholars of King's College, Cambridge 80, 136/7; Laing Art Gallery, Newcastle-on-Tyne 95; National Gallery of Scotland 46; National Museum of Wales 48 (right); National Portrait Gallery 48 (left), 86, 117, 125, 128/9, 130, 135; National Trust 51, 54, 75, 82, 83, 90, 111, 114; Sotheby's, London 6, 76, 85, 109, 124; Southampton City Art Gallery 142; Frances Spalding 13, 15, 36, 68, 115, 126, 133; Tate Gallery Archive (Vanessa Bell Albums) 19, 22, 28, 29, 37, 39, 44, 45, 52, 121 (right), 136; University of Hull Art Collection 2; University of Sussex Library (Monk's House Papers) 8, 53.

The work of Duncan Grant is © 1978 Estate of Duncan Grant, by kind permission of Paul Roche and Henrietta Garnett.